T0065172

JUST WHEN YOU *Thought* YOU KNEW

PAUL JONES

Order this book online at www.trafford.com
or email orders@trafford.com

Most Trafford titles are also available at major online book retailers.

Print information available on the last page.

ISBN: 978-1-6987-1410-3 (sc)
ISBN: 978-1-6987-1409-7 (hc)
ISBN: 978-1-6987-1411-0 (e)

Library of Congress Control Number: 2023903034

Trafford rev. 02/17/2023

www.trafford.com
North America & international
toll-free: 844-688-6899 (USA & Canada)
fax: 812 355 4082

Contents

Just When You Thought You Knew

Because this is not a perfect world, and we're not perfect people, we live and encounter many different things and adventures in our lives. Some might have nightmares while others might have had a very tough childhood that so often bleeds over to their adult lives. There are even those who think that they know it all and what's good for them.

Rather, you just want to be helped, or you want to be loved. The stories in this book will set you on an adventure, from fantasy to nightmares to dreams; and to some, it feels like the author was in the house with you. Welcome to your life stories, *Just When You Thought You Knew.*

A Nightmare to Live

One night while lying in bed, I had what seemed to be a dream. A dream where I had little to nothing to gain or to give.

And then I went back to sleep, and I soon discovered that it was not a dream at all but a nightmare to live!

I thought I woke up in the middle of the night.

The moon was shining, big and bright. I looked into the woods, and there was a glow.

Where was it coming from? I don't practically know. I looked across the meadow and then over to the creek. And then I saw what I thought was a human; he began to creep.

I soon woke up and walked across the floor. I had to wake up because I began to snore.

As I sat down, I began to think; but back into a deep sleep, I began to sink.

All of a sudden, I began to dream. It was really weird; so it would seem.

I saw some eyes looking at me; they began to stare. Once again, I had a thought that this might just be a nightmare.

I went outside and begun walking around, and then I was hit by a vehicle and knocked to the ground.

I thought to myself that everything was fine. But what I didn't realize was that something was wrong with my mind.

All of a sudden, in my mind I started to wake. It felt like my house was shaking; it felt like an earthquake.

I ran to the window, and the world as I knew it had changed. There were bombings, killings, and so much pain. I looked at the ground, and there wasn't an empty spot to be found.

There was a cold chill that came over me, for there was no one else left as far as I could see. I wondered, *How did I stay here? How did I survive? Am I the only one who's still alive?*

The days would go by, much like the nights. I often wondered if there had been a war, if there had been a fight? The days were very dim, much like the night; you could not tell one from the other because there wasn't much light.

I slowly gathered the nerves to venture out. What I stumbled on was enough to make a grown man scream, a grown man shout. The people whom I thought were my friends and the people whom I knew as my kin, they were all gone. I mean their bodies were decomposed all the way to their bones.

I slowly looked around for others to greet, but there seems to be no one else there for me to meet. I thought to myself, *This surely can't be right. What could have happened to make everyone to disappear from out of sight?*

A noise came from the woods. I wondered, *What was this that I heard?* I was really disturbed. My knees started to shake, and my stomach started to ache. I tried to take off and run. I tried to take off and sprint, but it was like my feet were stuck deep down in cement. I looked around to see what I could see, but all that I saw was a figure standing there, looking like a tree.

I made it back to my house. I could no longer call it my home because now I stayed there all alone. I once had lots of servants beckoning to my every will. I lived high on the hog. I was king of the hill.

I ran to the window. In my hands, I had a gun or two; but if something was to come at me, I couldn't say that I would know what to do. The palms of my hands were drenched with sweat. I hardly could hold my guns because my hands were soaking wet. While looking out my window, I didn't see anything. Things had quieted down; so it would seem.

I thought that it was over, but then all of a sudden, I felt this hand on my shoulder. Not even turning around, I smelled this awful stank; the odor was so bad I thought that I would faint. I slowly turned around, and much of a surprise to me, what stood there was a dead person looking like a zombie! I couldn't help but to think that he wanted to eat my brain, but then I thought to myself, *Am I just going insane?*

I quickly ran down the hall across the old wooden floor. I ran into the closet and closed the old wooden door. My heart was beating so hard. It really started to pound. It was so loud that I thought he would have heard the sound.

After about an hour or two, I finally got the nerves to take a peek. I thought to myself, *Is this all a dream? Am I really asleep?* I slowly walked into my room to look at my bed. I wasn't there; all I saw were some messed-up covers instead. I wondered if this could be a dream of me having a nightmare. Dream or not, this has put some fear in me; this has given me a scare.

There was no food in the house, nor was there anything to drink. I even tried to get some water out of the kitchen sink. I knew that I would soon have to go back out. I wished I had someone to go out before me, you know, just to scout.

I put one foot out the front door, and the board on the porch started to squeak. It squeaked so loud I thought that, in my pants, I might have leaked. I managed to hold what little that I had in as I walked a crossed the lawn down to the street. There was not another person there, not a one that I could meet.

I made it to what used to be a town; it was so sad to see as I looked around. I knew that I had to hurry and find some food for my plate because the sun was about to go down; it was getting kind of late.

In the open, I didn't want to be trapped; even though I carried my guns, I was good and strapped. Deep down inside, things just didn't feel right. I knew that I had to be going. I had to get out of sight. I saw this building; it was an abandoned jail. I quickly ran inside; it stunk like hell. I locked the door, and I boarded the windows. To make it even quieter, I walked on the pillows.

I heard these sounds coming from outside. I ducked down so low. I really tried to hide. When I peeped outside, I saw more zombies, and I knew if I had made some noise, they would have been coming for me. Then I heard this scream. It was the scream of a woman; so it would seem. Once again, I thought, *Was this a dream, or was this a nightmare?* I thought, *Should it really matter, or should I really care? But what if it really was a woman? Should I really care? Should I open the door and take a risk? Should I even dare?*

It wasn't like I knew who it was or where she might be, but was it just the fear building up inside of me? A coward all of my life, I have truly been; but could I not help her, only if she would scream again. Everything went silent. I didn't hear another sound. I thought, *Did the zombies find her? Was she found?*

Once again, I started to peep out the window; and much to my surprise, I saw her ducking down in a vehicle, ducking down inside. I wanted to make a dash for her and bring her inside with me, but the streets were full of the living dead; the streets were filled of zombies.

How could this be? How could I even care? I was truly hoping and praying that this was only a nightmare! I wanted to yell. I wanted to scream. But if I did that, I might had found out that this wasn't only just a bad dream.

I looked across the street into the car; she was so close, yet she was so far. I was hoping that she would do like me and just sit tight; maybe then it would all be over with the first sunlight.

All I could do was sit here and pray; it seemed like it was forever, before the break of day. The break of day came, and the zombies, they were still there. The sunlight didn't matter to them; they didn't even care.

How could they be such mindless freaks, yet they still care enough to kill and to eat? Then I saw my old dog; he ran down the street. I knew if they followed him, with her I could meet.

The zombies saw the dog, and they began to follow. I then took one deep breath, and my fear I tried to swallow. I opened the door, and I peeped to the left and to the right. I looked long and hard. I looked until they were out of my sight. I ran to the car that was across the street. I took one good look in the front and then into the back seat. It didn't take long for our eyes to meet.

She held a gun, and she pointed it at me; she asked, *Are you for real, or are you just another zombie?* I told her we must be going; we need to get out of these streets because a little dog is not much for so many zombies to eat!

To my house we decided to walk. We were as quiet as possible; we didn't even talk. We arrived at my house. And what stood in the door, it had to be one of those creatures, and he stood at least seven foot four. I looked to my left, and I saw my old hound; his eyes were fiery red. I thought then and there that I was hell bound. I looked at her, and for the first time, I saw her true feature. She was no human; she was one of those living dead creatures. I took off running, but where would I go? Everyone that I once knew, they were dead as far as I could know. I finished by lying on the ground and covering my head, but when I again opened my eyes, I was lying in my bed.

I looked around my room with such a stare, and I decided that the adventure that I just had had all been nothing but a living nightmare.

Making it Through The Pain

I have a question. How would you feel if one morning you woke up, and you found out that a friend had died? Oh, not by natural causes, but by his own hands; yes, I'm talking about suicide.

Not because of the pressures of life that he wanted to hide but from all of the emptiness down—deep, deep down—inside. Not because he felt like he didn't have anything to gain but from all of the physical hurt, the emptiness and pain.

They tried to dope him up with a lot of pills; they even tried to dope him up against his very own will.

If he died today, the world wouldn't even care; the world wouldn't even know, and those who thought knew him, some would even put on a show. Oh, some will laugh, and some will cry. But for most, they won't even have a tear in their eye. For those who knew him but never called, after a month or two, they probably won't even think of him at all.

The torment of his mind, the torment of his brain, is enough to make anyone go insane.

In his mind and his heart, he carries such a heavy load; it's enough to make one's head explode. They try to say that he just needs something to do, which in a way, you can say, is probably true.

But what will you do when that event comes to an end, and there is no one to reach out to, not even a friend?

Some people just say that you're just weak, but they're not able to look into your mind; they can't even take a peek.

For years, he severed his country, and he helped protect the citizens while most take this for granted or take it as a given. From the blood on his hands to the torment of his brain, makes him wonder how he stayed sane.

He had songs in his heart and music in his ears, but the sound of gunfire made the music not too clear. He wanted to stop the bullets. He wanted to stop the gunfire. He wanted to stop the pain. That was his heart's desire.

The rain of bullets came down in the heat of the night. Most ran for cover; some just got out of sight.

In his mind, he hears a child cry; the child cries because his mother is lying on the street corner about to die.

He thinks that this is a doll that he has just found, but it turns out to be a dead baby lying on the ground. He looks at this person, which happens to be a childhood friend. But now he's on the ground, covered with blood, and his life has just come to an end. He listens to a guy, and he says that his life, he's about to bring to an end. But this doesn't happen just once but again and again.

From as long as you can remember, the negativity started to form, yes, from the very moment that he was born. Just like some were born in the month of June, some were born into a family and fed with a silver spoon.

How can you say that these are true words that you speak by saying that a certain person's mind is not strong, that it is just weak?

A man wakes up every day, and his body starts to ache. And then he has to deal with those who say, "Oh, he's just a fake." The pain in his body, it hurts so bad. And then he has to listen to all the ones in power, and he gets mad.

Just to be heard, he begins to raise his voice. He feels like he has no other option; he has no other choice. He hurts so bad; he wants it all to end. He would do it himself, but he thinks that it's a sin.

He sits in the house alone; he tries to call someone up on the phone. He feels like he has nothing left; at this point, he'll talk to anyone, even to himself. He feels like he has nothing left inside; he feels like all he had, all he's done, has just dried up and died.

He's surrounded by his family, but there's still the emptiness; he asks, "Where is the joy? Where is the happiness?"

Through all of the hurt and pain, he still feels like he has so much to gain. He looks into that little one's eyes, and he gets such a warm feeling deep down inside. He remembers he said that he wouldn't put too much on you, and from that moment, he knows that he can pull through.

Just like the weather that will change, he still has the emptiness, the hurt, and the pain.

Just like he knows his word to be true, and he knows that he will never give up on you. He makes up his mind and calls his name, hoping that things in his life will definitely change.

The sky is blue one day, and then comes the rain. Things in his life will never be the same. He decided to live his life the best that he can. He doesn't get his hope too high; he doesn't make too many plans. He knows that there will always be joy and pain, but he also knows that there is always plenty to gain.

Today, it was cloudy, and the rain came down. But he kept his head above the waters; he didn't drown. The sun soon started to shine, and all of the rain and clouds were left behind. He soon went outside, and he was able to see; he thanked the Lord by saying, "Thank you, Lord, for shining down on me."

In This City

John was an old farmer from out of town. He thought that he would go to the city to look around.

He had been there a few years ago, so he thought that the sites and scenery he would know. He got on the bus and then the train; but as he got closer, he saw that the city, it had really changed.

John saw crime was around every corner and on every street in this city. There were no children playing nor sunlight shining in this city. Even the creatures and critters that once ruled the night, now they only appear in very dim light in this city.

John had planned to stay there for about a week, but he couldn't find the thing that he was looking for, the thing that he came to seek. You see, it's just him and his animals on his farm; he was hoping that he could find him a nice lady for him to charm.

Here, a day may come; a day may pass. But one wouldn't be able to tell one day from the last in this city. He couldn't believe a place like this; it was once prolific in progress, but now it is filled with turmoil and depression in this city.

Out on his old farm, the sun didn't cease to shine; he couldn't believe that he came here and left all of that behind. He used to wake up and smell the fresh morning grass; it would be enough to let him know that another day had come, and another day had passed.

But here, clouds are always in the sky; and most of these humans, they look like they're just hoping to die in this city. He looks around, and there is plenty water but none to drink because it is filled with dead animal corpses and stinks in this city.

On his farm, he used to put in a good day of work; he might have been sore, but no one was really hurt. John didn't realize that he had it so good; he would give anything to be back there now if he could. The person that said that the grass is greener on the other side, he didn't tell the truth; as a matter of fact, he just flat out lied.

John had only been here for a few days, and he saw that living here is not easy. In fact, it can be hard; for those who stay here, it can even be a job in this city. They have to do all they can to stay alive; heck, they might have to outright kill to survive in this city.

He couldn't forget the smell of his morning cup of coffee or the smell of his old cedar tree or even the smell that his old farm animals would leave behind; it was enough to put a smile on his face, to make his day shine.

Just him thinking about going out to his garden and getting himself some farm fresh tomatoes or him just walking around, with mud between his toes.

Here, there is such an awkward smell; it is enough to make a person think that they were in hell in this city. John saw them digging in garbage; some have to dig really deep just to make sure that they have enough to eat in this city.

He saw that here, only the strong know how to survive. They have the might; they are the only ones who know how to fight in this city.

No, he didn't think that he would stay here any longer. He felt a strong pull for his farm; he felt such a hunger.

He's going to try and get out of here as quick as he can because this place is not fit for neither beast nor man in this city. John just needs to make it out of his room and across the town without getting punched, mugged, or just getting knocked down. In this city.

Wait a minute. John saw this lady, and she appeared to be what he wanted her to be; she was pleasant to his eyes as far as he could see. But what about the two guys behind the wall? Does she think that he's that stupid? For an old trick like this, does she think that he would fall? In this city.

John quickly hurried up his pace; he didn't want to leave a trace. He wanted to shake the dust from his feet; he wanted to make a hasty retreat.

If he had to run all the way back to his farm, at least there, he knew that his animals would do him no harm.

He took off running, trying to make the bus, but the bus didn't stop' he wanted to cuss in this city.

He saw this bike just lying on the ground; he picked it up as if it was in lost and found in this city. John got on the bike and pedaled as fast as he could. He pedaled down the street through alley, and finally, he made it into the woods.

He knew that he had a lot of miles to go, and then a funny thing happened; it started to snow. He was just happy to be out of that city.

The wind started blowing; it got really cold. It was so cold that his face froze. He knew that he had to get off that bike and find some heat; he saw this building, but when he walked in, he felt like a piece of meat.

They looked at him as if they were cannibals; they looked at him like he was a freshly killed animal. John quickly turned around and got the heck out of there. He'll deal with the cold weather; he didn't even care.

After miles of running and walking, he made it back to his farm. He thought to himself, *It was truly an adventure, but there was no harm. I know the next time that I want to feel sorry for myself and I want some pity, there is one trip I won't make, and that trip is to the city.*

He soon saw his neighbor walking down the old dirt road. She was carrying a bushel; she was carrying a load. He thought, *She has never looked that good to me. I guess I should have just opened my eyes, and then I might have been able to see.*

He ran to her and asked if he could help her carry her load.

She replied, "I heard that you went to the city to find a wife; this I was told." He bulked his eyes and held his head down to the ground because he knew that in that city, there wasn't a wife to be found.

He quickly made up his mind; he tried to throw out some lines. "Yes, into the city I went, and I thought I would find, I thought I would find, someone whom I could make mine, but if I had just opened my eyes, I would have been able to see that the woman whom I truly needed lives right next door to me. I have had to walk about a mile or two, but it will all be worth it if I could get you to say I do."

She looked into his eyes as he held her hand; he finally figured out what she knew all of the time, that is, he was meant to be her husband. He looked at her from head to toe, that beauty and side of her he thought he would never know.

At last, he thought to himself, *It surely was a pity that I thought that I had to find me a wife in that city.*

Just The Three of Us

The thoughts in his mind, you thought you knew, but did you really know him? Did you know what was true?

If you were able to look into his mind, what would you see? A garden, a yard, or maybe even a tree. Or is his life a complete mystery?

The tears that run down his face, do they not give you a clue? Are they tears of joy, or are they tears because he's really blue?

The words that he speaks, are they words that you can trust, or are they just simply words of lust? You try so hard to look him in his eye. Will that give you the answers you're looking for? Why do you even try?

You say that he's playing little games, yet you turn around and do the exact same. You don't really know him at all, yet it's his number that you continue to call.

You act like you were surprised when you finally saw the evil that was inside. He did all he could do to push you away, yet you insisted; you decided to stay. You said you could make him the man that you wanted him to be; he tried to warn you, but the true him you thought you wanted to see.

You two dated for two, almost three, years; and all he ever made you do was to shed a lot of tears. Why in the world did you continue to hold on? You've done all you could to make him your husband, but he begged you to stop; he even tried to demand.

Could you not tell that something was wrong with his brain? Could you not tell that he was a bit insane?

He grew up and had a very hard life; he didn't know how to treat you even after he had made you his wife. There was no father in his house to teach him how to be a man; even if it was, he still doesn't think that he can.

You know, just like a tree that blows in the wind, he was truly hoping that you two could have remained as friends.

He wishes that you could be heard; he often misses all of your kind words, the way you used to speak to him, the way things used to be, the way you used to come home from work, how you used to fix his plate and place his spoon and fork. You didn't even care if he stayed home all day, and when you got paid, you even gave him more than half of your pay.

Who was this guy named Stan? Your husband tried to tell you that we were jealous men! Was he the one who tried to take our place? Yeah, we got rid of him without a trace! We didn't like the way that you looked at Stan; you made us feel like he was your other man.

You thought that we three had a perfect life, but now we stand here with this knife! We slashed Stan's throat; that was just the start. Now it's your turn; we're about to cut out your heart!

Why did you make us do this?

Because we know that when you're gone, you will be truly missed. We have to do this to teach you not to cheat; the mistake that you made, you will not be able to repeat!

Don't you ask dare ask us about our child; you think we're going to just let him grow up wild? When we're finished with you, we're going to take care of him too!

We guess you're happy now; we stand here with your blood and your heart in our hands. You had to mess things up; you had to force us to kill Stan! You had to mess with our feelings; you had to make us care! If only you truly knew us, if only you were only aware!

Just look what you made us do.

Another Lonely Night

Here she is spending another lonely night; she thought that you would be here to hold her tight. You had her to move here from her home state, and now she set here staring at an empty plate.

When we use to talk on the phone, you told her that you wanted her here with you; you wanted her for your own. And now that she's here, she can only see you at her place; all the words that you said have now been erased.

You told her that you had an ex-wife; you said that she was no longer a part of your life. But then one day, you completely let it slip; you said that you and she had taken a trip.

She thought that she meant so much to you, but now she doesn't know what to do. She left all of her peace that she once had within to find out that she was coming here to live in sin. From all of her loneliness, she tried to flee for you to simply do this at this degree.

She might have a lot of problems in her life, but she can happily say that she's certainly glad that she's not your wife. She knew that you tried to put the move on her; she just wonders how many more women that you have tried to explore.

She doesn't know your wife, but she's sure that she's a pretty good woman; she has to be to deal with this life. She just happened to married a good-for-nothing man. I'm not going to stand here and talk about you because I was willing to get with you. I'm just telling you the truth.

She thought to herself, *Here I am spending another lonely night. I thought he would be here to hold me tight. I thought since my feelings were so strong, there was no way he could treat me wrong. I gave him all the love that I had, yet I'm still here feeling empty and sad. I even got up and made him breakfast in bed when I should have been kicking him out instead. I guess to him this was just another lustful affair, and I truly thought that he really cared. One day he too will be all alone; then and only then will he learn to appreciate what he has at home, yet I still lay here burning with desire without his or anyone's love to quench my fire. He might be thinking that here I will always be, that I'm waiting for him to decide, that he wants to be with me. But this is the end of him; he will definitely see!*

Yet she goes to work with a smile on her face; because of the emptiness, she tries not to leave a trace. She works hard and tries not to let her pain show. It's no one's else business; it's not for them to know.

I know that the tears in her eyes she had to shed, but she knew that she had too much in her to beg. She knows that what you've done was so wrong, but she knows in her heart that she is very strong.

You or this world will never get the better of me. I will continue to come out on top; you will see. Whether you see or not, I don't really care; I'll just toss this up as a really bad nightmare. I'm going to go ahead and continue on with my life and I suggest that you move on and continue on with your wife. If you can live with your life, I can live with mine because I know sooner or later, my love I will find.

She has known pain before, but each time after that pain, there was another door. She's tired of talking to you, so this is goodbye; but one thing that she must say: don't ever come back this way; don't even try.

Lord, now that he's gone, I turn to you; my heart is broken again. I don't know what to do. You know when I came out here, I thought I was doing the right thing. He was good and kind; so it would seem. I know what I did was a big sin, but Lord, you saved me yet again. I will continue on with my life although something inside is telling me to end it with a knife. I will pick myself up and not listen to that voice that's inside because if I had listened to that voice, I would have truly died. Lord, I really don't know what to say. I do know that I need to seriously get on my knees and pray.

Another year has come, and now it's gone; she can honestly say this is her new home.

Friends she tried to make, she even decided to go on other dates. She wants to get married and to make a home; she doesn't enjoy living her life, her life, all alone. But for now, she goes to work and comes back to an empty apartment; she has decided that she'll just wait for her man who will be Godsent.

Eugene

Let me introduce you to Eugene. Eugene is a superhero; no, he doesn't leap tall buildings in a single bound, but his feet are planted on solid ground. Yes, he has made a lot of mistakes in his life; he has even gotten divorced from at least one or two wives.

Eugene is a superhero.

With his children, he probably wasn't all that great, but he always made sure that they had enough food on their plates. With the neighbors, he tried to be the best that he could; he was well respected in his neighborhood.

Eugene is a superhero.

Eugene has not always been such a positive figure; he once was known to drink a lot of liquor. He didn't get drunk and raise a lot of hell, but because of his drunkenness, a lot of his projects didn't make it; a lot of his projects just fail. Once he got divorced, a lot of women he did see; he often thought, *One or two women isn't enough for me.*

Eugene is a superhero.

Eugene used to work as a security guard; when he first started there, it was kind of hard. He had a problem with them walking around and saying that they were forgiven of their sins; he thought,

So now you think that in heaven, you're going to get in? Eugene knew that those who were locked up had a lot of scars, but he thought, *I probably too have scars if I had to live my life behind bars.*

Eugene is a superhero.

Eugene tried to help a lot of people around his neighborhood. He even cooked for some; oh, he could cook pretty good. He taught some kids how to fly a kite; he even taught some how to ride their bikes. When he did his lawn and cut his grass, he would cut the elderly's lawn with three or four passes.

Eugene is a superhero.

Eugene had one old friend with whom he used to hang around; his friend was one of those who probably would be listed in the lost and found. He was one of those friends who really didn't think highly of himself, but he would go out of his way for everyone else. Eugene hung around with him; sometimes, they would fish, and at other times, Eugene would just cook and take him a dish.

Eugene is a superhero.

Eugene had some sons, and he did all that he could; he wishes that he could have done more, and if he was given a chance, he would. He taught his sons how to fish and to have fun; he even taught the proper use for a gun. He taught them that it was okay for a man to show love, but he wishes that he had taught them more about the Lord up above.

Eugene is a superhero.

Eugene was a man who kept a lot of feelings deep down inside, so on the morning that he was found, there was no surprise that he had died. Eugene was not a very brave man, but he pretended, pretended like so many of us can. Eugene lived a pretty good life, but when they rolled him over, in his stomach was a knife. He did not leave a letter; he just left this note. On this piece of paper, these are the words that he wrote:

I had a good life, but I had a lot of pain. I hope that others will go get some help and not walk around like me, walk around insane.

Eugene was a superhero.

Living in Fear

When in your head you begin to live in fear, you know in your heart that fear is always near. Peace is somewhat hard to find when you try to find it deep in your mind. Your life might not be the best, but you can happily say that you're not worse off than the rest. You close your eyes, and the images that you see let you know that the world will never be what you hope it to be.

The ship had just sailed. But the water is pouring in, and now you must bail. The sun is high in the sky, and your mouth is good and dry. You want to drink the water that you see, but inside you think, *This water is not good for me.*

On the water, the rain starts to fall; you open your mouth, and try to catch it all. The clothes on your back are getting soaked. You drank too much water; you begin to choke. All of a sudden, your stomach starts to growl; you're so hungry you hang your head over the bow. The fish swim by, and they look at you. You don't have a pole or hook; you don't know what to do.

The waves start to toss you high and low; where they're taking you, you don't rightly know. You see the lows, and you see the caps; if only you could have lain down and taken a nap.

You walk around the corner with a gun in your hand; the fear you had was only a shadow and not a man. You try not to walk on a crack because you heard that if you do, you could break your mother's back. You see another person walking by; they try to speak, but you're so afraid, all you do is sigh.

You make it to the store, and you pull out your money; you get afraid because you think that the other customers are looking at you funny. You then put your change back into your pockets so deep; then you make it back home, and you don't come back out for weeks.

Your girlfriend asks you to go for a ride; you sneak out of your house and get into her car and try to hide. She asks you, "Why are you so afraid?" You tell her, "Last night, you watched a movie called *Blade*." She asks, "So you think there are vampires here to suck your blood?" You answer, "It's raining an awful lot. Do you think that it might flood?"

You and your girl go out to eat; you look at the food as if there is something wrong with the meat. She asks, "Do you want something to drink?" You reply, "Do you think they wash this dishes in a clean sink?" You and she start to fuss, and then she gets up and walks out because she has had enough.

To get back home, you must take the bus. But some other guys got on, and they started to cuss. You get so afraid because one of them has a knife; you think, *Is this the end, the end of my life?* They look at you straight into your eyes; you were so afraid you wanted to cry. The bus made it to your stop, but when you stood up, it felt like your heart dropped.

When he made it back into his home, he locked all seven locks on his door; he even placed a bar under the knob, down to the floor. He looked around in every room, and then he sat there all alone, thinking that the world will soon be doomed.

He refuses to call his girl on the phone; he would rather sit in his house looking at the walls all alone. He once had a pet, but he thought that it was going mad. So he went to the vet and had it put to sleep; so sad. All of a sudden, his phone starts to ring; there's hope for him; so it would seem. He doesn't pick up the phone, yet he's still depressed; he didn't pick up because he thought that it might be the IRS.

He has a car parked in his drive. He doesn't go anywhere in it; he's too afraid that he might never arrive. He once saw this movie where the car blew up at the station, so he has decided to stay at home and never go on vacation. A bunker in the ground is where he has decided to live. Is this guy fiction? Is this guy for real?

He was so afraid. He had a girl, but every time she got too close, he would push her away. But then he would turn right around and beg her to stay. She soon got tired of his love being off and on; he woke up one morning, and he was all alone. She left him a note. "It's not your fault. You're not to blame, but you do need to get some help because I think that you're a bit insane."

John went outside to go to get a bite to eat. He passed by everyone, looking at the ground; he was afraid to speak. He made it to the restaurant; he walked inside. The server asked, "How may I help you?" It took about thirty minutes before he replied. Nervously, he said that he would like a snack, a quarter pounder with cheese and a Big Mac.

John had this delusion that when things got bad, it was better to live in seclusion. He thought that when he got depressed, being alone was the best. He would go to work and do all of those things, which he thought was okay; so it would seem. John didn't realize that he was letting himself go; he thought that no one else would know. He thought that he could handle the situation all by himself. He thought that he didn't need any help; he didn't need anyone else.

One day, the pressure of living became too great, John made one final mistake. He decided that he no longer wanted to live, so he opened up a bottle and took a lot of pills. But the pills in the bottle didn't take his life away, but now in a nursing home, he has to stay. He is no longer able to think and do for himself; all he can do is to depend on everyone else.

As black men, we have to learn to take care of not only our bodies but also our minds. Some of us find that so hard to do. The stress and strain that we go through of just being black, from dealing with competing with our counterparts to racial profiling to trying to provide for our families, and that's only naming a few. We must learn that alcohol, gambling, sex, and violence are not the answer for all things.

So many of us have deep-suppressed issues, but we refuse to seek help; we think that seeking help is a sign weakness or that others will think that we're crazy. We care more about our jobs and about what others might think than we do about ourselves when sometimes, all you might need is to get the thoughts that are lingering in your heart and head out. Yes, I do know that our God can and will work things out; but this is why he has given us resources, people who are trained to listen and to give advice.

Black men, not only black men but all men, if help is needed, seek help!

The Mind of A Maniac

Because the wind blew away from Little Larry's house, a fresh odor filled the air. Little Larry was a mischievous little child, and overall, he was just growing up wild.

He was a happy child because he didn't know how bad he had it. His name is Larry, and he lived on a hog farm. He had hogs as far as the eye could see, and he knew that they would cause him no harm.

They say that he was a happy child. But as they look back over his life, one can honestly say that his childhood was not as happy, and it was filled with strife.

He remembers growing up, like most of the children today, without a father and a lot of times, they would just go astray.

He used to see his mother come home with different guys. But by the morning, they would leave, and he would stand there with tears in his eyes. He would run back into his room pretending that he was still asleep; he had no idea that his memories would still hunt him not only for days but for several weeks.

He remembers lying in bed at night hearing his mother in her bedroom, making all kind of sounds. Even today as a young man, he still has visions of men lying on top of his mother, messing around, and then only seeing her waking up once again all alone without a second visit or even a call on the phone.

Little Larry, it's time to get up.

So he would get up, not mentioning anything about the person that she came home with the night before, but he remembered the moment that person left out of the front door.

Larry, you know that we have to get out there and slop those hogs. He was oh too happy to throw on his old pair of coveralls.

He guessed that was a way for him to get away from that environment where he didn't want to stay. He often thought that he was all alone on this earth from the moment he was conceived until his birth.

He remembers the time his mother's female friend came over; she leaned over and whispered in his ear over his shoulder. She and his mother were drinking and listening to music and having fun; she looked at him and said that she wanted to give him some. He was using the bathroom, and she came in; she said that she wanted to be his special friend. He didn't know what she was going to do; his eyes got wide, and then she took his hand and placed it in her deep inside. He did not know that would also affect him for the rest of his life even when he wanted to get married and to get a wife.

He was very young when this event took place, but the memories in his mind, he cannot erase. He went over to a babysitter because his mom wanted to go out; the babysitter had a daughter, and she was beginning to sprout. The daughter immediately took a liking to him. She was a little older; she stood naked in front of him, and then she bent over. She was a little older and more advanced; then she said to him, this is your lucky chance. They played for a while, and then she told him to lie on his back; she then took his little man out and put it in her mouth as if it was a snack. She did things to him, and it felt so good; she did things that he didn't think a person could. He still thinks about that too.

His young life was not all about those types of things. He did have somewhat of a childhood, whether or not it may seem.

He was told things like he was dumb and things like he was a bastard's son. He was also told that he was crazy, and then they would often say that he was good for nothing because he was too lazy. He was told that he was too weak because all of his personal business, he decided to keep. The things that he did, he didn't like to share. So that made him weak, but he didn't care.

You know things that would hurt or affect a so-called normal kid but not Larry. And you sit here and wonder why his mind slid.

They say that he's a maniac just because he raped his first person at the young age of ten, and it felt so good to be in control, he would do it all over again and again. He thinks he's normal. He's just a product of his environment; he just delt with the hand that he was sent.

He was taught that's what life is all about. He loved to hear his victims when they would shout.

He loved little children, those he would never harm; for some reason, it reminded him of his little pigs down on his farm. He liked sitting in the parks watching the families, the moms and dads; they seemed like they were so happy. It took away the thoughts of his young life, which was so crappy.

He often mentions of having a very happy childhood, a mom and dad, who would do all the things just like they should.

He would say, "Mom and Dad were a loving pair. They loved me so much. They really cared."

We were so happy.

My dad used to place me on his knee, and he used to read to me. For Christmas, I got lots of presents. He remembers the year that he got a BB gun. It was just like the one on that movie; he had a lot of fun.

Larry often thinks that he's someone else; he often talks like he's not himself.

He remembers that once he set a building on fire, he wanted to watch the flames so that he could admire.

There was this family of cats in there; he watched them burn. He watched them trying to get out; he watched the churn. They burned like they were meat on the grill, yet there was no sadness that he would feel.

We asked him, "Why did you do it?" He said the answer is simple; he just didn't give a sh—!

Larry's mind often drifts; he's not trying to deceive, but it's up to us, what statements we choose to believe.

He says he had a dog growing up; they were best friends. He loved that dog all the way until the end. He said that one day, he took him into the woods and told him to stay, so he cut his legs off so he wouldn't run away. He said that he loved his dog with of his heart; once he cut his legs off, he used to pull him around in his cart.

But then he said that he could not have a pet as a child; his mom once told him that he was too crazy, and he was too wild. His mom told him that we could not have a pet because they were too poor. She wasn't very nice, but he loved her even the more.

He said that is why he killed her first. He said that she looked so nice with that smile on her face; he said that he wanted to jump into the coffin, and that smile he wanted to erase.

He said that he has some words; he said that he wants to be heard.

And now I'm sitting here on death row. Why? Because they say that I killed some folks. So why do they also say that I'm insane? If I'm insane, how can I be sitting here on death row? Am I to blame?

I once caught this cat; it was around the Fourth of July. I took a firecracker and stuck it up his crack. I lit it, and it went boom. The cat ran away and flew into the air, but he came back down again soon.

So you ask me, how many people have I killed? I do not have to count. I don't feel like I have killed anyone. I feel like I just stopped them from breathing, and besides, I was just having fun!

Let's Talk

One day, a mother sat down and had a talk with her daughter. When I first saw this boy, I thought he was so fine; I just knew that I had to make him mine. He was just fifteen, but I thought I could be his pretty little queen. I was just a student in the sixth grade, and I had perfect grades. I made all As.

I made a mistake and told him how I feel, but at that time, I thought it was no big deal. He pulled me to the side and whispered "I love you," but I didn't realize that he just wanted to do the do.

Just remember, I was just in the sixth grade and only eleven; he told me to meet him at his house around about seven. I told my mom that I was going to my friend's, and from that very moment on, all of my innocence would end.

From the moment I got there, he started to kiss and hug; then he put his hand in my pants, and he started to rub. Before I could tell him to stop, I felt my pants and my underwear drop. He told me to turn around and to bend over. I then felt his hands up on my shoulder, which I thought was very strange; and then all of a sudden, I felt so much pain. I wanted to run. I wanted to hide, but then it felt like something was pouring in me deep down inside.

He then pulled out and ran away. I didn't know if I should leave or if I should stay. I slowly stood up and fixed my clothes. I had tears streaming down my face and snot running out of my nose. I slowly walked home, thinking to whom I can I tell. I thought, *Here I am having sex. I'm not even twelve.*

Three months would go by, and I'm starting to show. I thought, *Can I keep this from my mom, or does she already know?*

I tried to call him and tell him what he had done; he said that he would call me back, that he was outside having fun. So I decided to wait by the phone; I thought, *He would call me back. It wouldn't take too long.*

I came to realize that all his sweet words weren't true. I was getting beside myself; I didn't know what to do.

My mom called out; we're going for a float. I started to run out the door, and I forgot my coat. I tried to turn around before she could see, but she wasn't fooled at all; she was there waiting for me. She said that it was hard enough raising us three and that she would help, but this baby would have to depend me.

Months seemed to drag by, and then it was September; something happened then, something that I would always remember. I thought before I could grow up and become a lady, I was going to the hospital to have my own baby.

But as you can see, I didn't let having you stop me.

I went back to school, and I still made all As. I wasn't going to work for any minimum wage.

And now for the man who's called your dad, I guess I should be angry; I should be mad.

But I can't be mad at him, and not at me too, because I realize that there are consequences for the things that we do.

It's just some of us learn from the things that we did, and some of us don't. I guess this is why he has eleven kids.

So before you find yourself starting an early family, I want you to know that you can always talk to me.

This is Serious

Billy was sitting at his desk at school; you know, the place where they used to teach the golden rule.

The officer walked in, the one whom most of the students considered as their friend. He told them that they were going to have an active shooter drill. Billy jumped up and screamed, "Man, is this for real?"

Billy thought to himself, *Why should we have an active shooter's drill here at school? This has to be against policy. It has to be against the rules.* He told the officer, "A drill like this is a waste of time. You should be on the streets where people are really dying!"

The officer looked and Billy and asked, "If someone was to come into this school and started to shoot, what would you do? Do you have an answer? Do you have a clue?"

Billy laughed, "Man, do you think that someone would be stupid enough to come in here and start to spray? There's too many of us. How would they get away?"

The officer said, "Young man, how many have to die, how many have to get killed, before you take this seriously and know that this can be for real? What do you watch on TV? Did you not see just the other night at least nineteen students suffered this tragedy?"

That is the reason why we have this mock so if something like this happens, you won't go into shock. This drill isn't only for you students; it's for the teachers too. They must know how to fight back, and at the same time try to stay calm, because they need to stay safe and help keep you all from bodily harm.

Once again, Billy laughed, "Man, I can take care of myself, and I can care less about anyone else."

"So you wouldn't care if someone was to come in here and shoot your classmates?"

"If he was to come in here, it would be one big mistake."

"Billy what do you mean? What would you do?"

"I know one thing that I wouldn't do, and that is to depend on you. I saw on television the other day where this guy went into this school, into one of the classrooms, and he started to spray. You guys came, and you just stood in the hallways. Shots continued to rain out, and kids continued to fall. So you tell me, why should I put my life into your hands because after all, you're just getting paid, and you're just a man?"

"Billy, I know of the shooting that you saw on TV, but I promise you that if anything like that happens here, that's not how it would be. I have to admit that those officers dropped the ball, and there is no way in hell, excuse me, there is no way that all of those students should have had to fall."

"Time after time, officers are brave. When they have a man down, they talk, hit, spray, and kick when they have a man on the ground. And when they're the only ones with guns, they're ready to shoot, but when others have guns, they have to go and make a plan they have to reboot. So you're telling me that I'm going to just all of a sudden forget all that you all have done and to put my life into your hands simply because you're a policeman?"

"Billy, I understand how you must feel, but all I can say is that things would or will be a lot different. I'm for real."

My Jewel

I simply thought that I had found my jewel once I moved out of the city and into the rural.

I have traveled all around the world, and I've seen a lot of pretty girls. Then I decided to go and look for one on this distant farm. I thought to myself, *What dangers could there be? Surely it can cause no harm.*

I arrived on the farm and stayed a day or two. It wasn't much like the city; there wasn't much to do. I saw some chickens, some horses, and even some cows; but then one day, I looked up, and I was in wow! I looked at your eyes, your feet, and your hair; it was enough to make me forget about all of my worries, all of my cares.

Then when you opened your mouth and said, "Howdy. How are you?" I questioned myself, *Could this be love? What should I do?* You grabbed my hand and asked if I wanted to ride. I then felt a deep sinking feeling in me deep down inside. You asked me if I needed help getting onto my saddle. You said, "It's easy. All you have to do is to straddle."

That day would go by much too fast. I wanted that day to never end; I wanted it to last. You asked me how long I was going to stay. I never wanted it to end; I never want to go away. It wasn't too long before I would ask you for your hand. I thought that I really wanted to be your husband.

All day long, at your beauty I would stare. I had no idea that my life would soon turn into a living nightmare! I did everything I could to keep you happy and to make you smile. I even went the extra distance. I went the extra mile!

When I first met you, I never wanted to let you go. I thought that our love was true; this I wanted to let you know. It was just like the dew that settled on the morning grass; I truly thought that our love was meant to last. If darkness was to fall, and I couldn't see, I would still feel good, just knowing that you would be here with me. It's like we're perfect; like two sets of hands inside gloves, we were meant to share this precious love. Just like when I plant this seed, and I watch it grow, our love is true; I want you to know. One thing I do know is that if I were to lose you, I won't say that my world would end; but one thing I do know is that if this happens, I'll know that I would have lost my true love and my best friend.

I should have never taken you off of the farm. Before I did that, our lives were dreamy; our lives were charmed. Now that you are here with me in this city, my life has gone to hell; what a pity! You act like you're a piece of meat in a butcher's shop, and all of your fooling and running around, you refuse to stop! I thought for sure that you living in the city would be a lot fun. I regret that I brought you here, and now I must say that I think that we are done!

Since we've gotten married and I've moved you here, my health has started to fade. I'm afraid that one day I'll awake, and to my throat, you'll be holding a blade. You used to say how much you loved me, but now, your presents I often long to see! Maybe to the farm I should take you back because here you're like a dope fiend who has found their first hit of crack!

You so often come home late at night, and then you sneak into the house, trying to stay out of my sight! I ask you to come and get into our bed. I even beg; I even plea! You must not forget that you are my wife, and it's you that I still want to see! Oh, I forgot you can have sex with everyone else, but you expect me to just take care of myself! I guess you know that you are leaving me with no other recourse. I'm simply asking you for a divorce!

Don't even look at me, and why is there a tear in your eye? I did everything that I could to keep us together, but you didn't even try. Your life could have been so glamorous, but you had to turn out to be so scandalous. What are you pulling out of your purse? What can you do to me to make my life even worse?

Oh, you want to pull a gun on me. Are you insane? This is the situation that you've created; you're the one to blame! Pull the trigger if you think that you can. I'm not going to beg. I'm not going to run. I'm simply going to stand. That's right; I thought you would put the gun down. Oh, so now you want to talk. Okay, I'll listen to every sound.

You want to be with me; this is what you want me to believe, or with these words that you're speaking, are you just trying to deceive? You ask me to come and hold you tight; no, for some reason, that just wouldn't feel right!

No, I think that I will ship you back to where I found you; maybe, yes, just maybe, one day, you'll find a love that you can hold on to! For now, here you can no longer stay. I just want you to go away!

No, you don't have to go back to the farm, but whomever you've been with, let's see if he'll let you rest in his arms. Don't get loud; don't cause a scene. But for now you must be on your way; but one thing's for certain, for you, I will always pray.

Now, that she's gone out into this world, I wonder was she only meant to be a simple farm girl? Am I the one to blame for bringing her with me and trying to make her change? All I wanted from her was to make her my wife; all I wanted was to give her a new life. I wonder if she would have turned out this way if on that farm. I would have just let her stay. Maybe the change was too extreme; maybe it was too much for her. You know what I mean? Maybe she was always this way; maybe I should have waited to see, but I thought that she was in love, in love with me.

Who am I fooling? I thought that I had found a jewel, but all I found was a girl trying to get out of the rural!

The Country Bumkins: First Day Back

The summer was over, and it was the first day of the last year of high school for our two country bumkins. As you might recall, PJ and DI had decided to stop being class clowns and to get serious with their schoolwork. But as so many might know, sometimes it's harder to turn over a new leaf, especially when so many have already labeled you.

DI. PJ, now that we're going to be smart, what do we do for fun? Are all our laughs and jokes done?

PJ. DI, we are going to be smart. Look, we still can have fun, and the jokes are not done. We can still be the guy on the block without being the laughing stock.

DI. Man.

PJ. Come on, DI. You will see. We can do it. You are very intelligent. You don't give yourself enough credit.

They both started to laugh.

DI. Man.

DI and PJ walked into the school. They looked on the wall, and it was plastered with all of the rules. Just as soon as they entered the first hallway, Chill Will headed their way.

Chill Will. Hey, DI, you ready for our last year? Man, I know we are going to have a lot of fun. We will make everyone cheer! Man, why you looking like that? You down with me? Now I know my old country bumkin is not going to let me down. We will see.

PJ. Chill, let me ask you something. What's your GPA? I bet it's kind of high, I would say?

Chill. PJ, why do you want to know? And if you don't get out of my face, I'm going to knock your butt to the floor.

PJ. If I was you, I'll step back before you get smacked. What's your GPA?

Chill. Well, I think it's around a 3.5 or 3.6. So DI, are you down? Let's split.

DI's mouth flew open.

PJ. That's what I thought. So why is it you're always trying to get my friend to act a fool for entertainment, but you're not willing to do the same? To you, he's just something to play with. He's just like a game.

Chill. Someone has to be the class clown. Are you down?

PJ. You got the wrong one, Chill. I'm not afraid of you, and if you don't back up, you're going to catch these two.

Chill punched PJ in the face. The fight was on. PJ hit Chill so many times and so fast that Will felt the last one, and then he felt the first.

The principal and some other teachers came and broke up the fight. They were taken to the office, and both were given a three-day suspension. PJ called his mother.

PJ. Hey, Mom, the principal wants to talk to you.

Mom. PJ, today is the first day. What did you do?

Principal. Yes, ma'am. PJ and another student were involved in an altercation, and for that, PJ will be suspended for three days. Any further altercations could result in expulsion, which means that PJ might not be able to graduate. Can you come and pick him up? PJ, go and have a seat. Your mother said that she was on her way to get you.

PJ. May I speak?

Principal. Go ahead, PJ. This is the first day. You haven't been here for a week.

PJ. First, I want to apologize for this fight, but you see, it was for our good. I would explain it to you if I could.

Principal. Your good? Who else was involved in it?

PJ. No, sir. No one else was involved in the fight, but DI and myself, we are trying to do a lot better this year. We are trying to do things right, and I wanted to show DI that those other guys and girls who all of the time laughed at us were just using us.

Principal. I understand what you were trying to do, but couldn't you have done that without the fight?

PJ. Well, it wasn't my intention to fight. It was kind of forced on me, and if you take a look at the cameras, you will see.

PJ went out to the outer officer, took a seat, and hesitantly waited for his mom to come. It seemed to take forever, but it also seemed like time was flying by. While he was sitting, he looked out the window and saw DI standing outside; he appeared to whisper, "I'm sorry." Just as PJ was about to reply, his mom walked in. He looked at her and dropped his head.

His mother didn't say a word. She walked to the secretary's desk and asked,

Mom. Is the principal in? If so, may I speak with him?

At that moment, the principal walked out.

Mom. Hello, Mr. Williams. I'm PJ's mother, and if you have a minute, I would like to speak with you.

Mr. Williams. Sure. Please come in. We definitely need to talk.

Mom. Mr. Williams, can you tell me what exactly happened?

Mr. Williams. Well, this is what I know. PJ told me that no one else was involved, but I do feel like he's not telling the whole story.

Mom. Mr. Williams, how do you feel about me possibly transferring PJ to another school?

Mr. Williams. Well, I can't suggest that you transfer or not. When parents tell me things like that, it kind of puts me on the spot.

Mom. Well, you see, Mr. Williams, PJ has this little friend. I know that he loves him, and they have lots of fun.

Mr. Williams. I know exactly the little guy. All of us around here call him DI.

Mom. DI, he loves to have fun. Oh, don't get me wrong. I love him, just like he was my son!

Mr. Williams. Ms. Martin, I really don't know about taking him away, but I do think that you should let him stay. PJ is not a bad student. It's not like he's impudent.

Ms. Martin. Oh, I know PJ had better be respectful because if he wasn't, he would be very regretful.

Mr. Williams. Ms. Martin, I can't tell you what to do with your child, but why don't you just take him home for now and think about it for a while.

Ms. Martin walked out of Mr. Williams's office and looked at PJ. He got up and walked behind her.

Mom. PJ, right now don't you say a word. This is not the time for you to try and to be heard.

PJ held his head down and continued to walk behind his mom. They made it to their car and started home, but his mom didn't go straight home. Instead, she took a different route. She drove by the boy's reform school.

Mom. PJ, look up. There is something I want you to see. Now you tell me, son, is this the place where you want to be?

PJ held his head up as he looked out the window. He saw guys so dark that they looked purple; they were in the scorching hot sun with sling blades, cutting the grass that grew on side of the roads. They were slopping hogs, throwing hay to cows, and doing all manners of free labor.

PJ. Momma, can I explain?

Mom. You had better make it good and make it plain.

PJ. Momma, I know that today is the first day of school. DI and myself, we were in the hall looking over the rules. Then this guy, Chill Will, came over, and he started to pick. He started treating us like clowns. He wanted us to do tricks. Then he punched me. I said then I can't let this be. Momma, you see, I had to defend us because I know in the past, we were a discuss.

Ms. Martin continued to drive; at first, she didn't say too much. They made it to their house.

Momma. PJ, come here, son. I have something to say. I was thinking about taking you out of that school, taking you away. Your dad lives over there. With him you could move, and then you can easily go to that other school.

PJ looked down with tears in his eyes.

PJ. Momma, please don't move me. You won't have any more trouble from me. At least I'll give it a try.

Momma. PJ, my dear, I understand that this is your last year. Have you
ever thought about what's going to happen when you walk across
that stage, when you and your friend DI have come of age?

Back at school, it was lunchtime. DI was walking around. He started
to think about his friend PJ; he started to think about all the things PJ
was talking about, about how all of the other students were just using
him and making fun of him. Right then, DI made up his mind.

Pebbles. Hey, DI, do you want to play? How about saying all of those
funny things that you used to say?

DI opened his mouth, and he begun to speak; but when the words
came out, Pebbles looked at him as if he was a circus freak.

Just like that, DI had made a change. From that moment on, he
was an ideal student; things were not the same.

The Country Bumkins: Going Their Separate Ways

The school year was quickly coming to an end; although they were at different schools, PJ and DI still remained friends. Every day after they made it home, they either talked in person or talked on the phone.

PJ. Hey, DI. How was your day?

DI. I'm on the football team, and I think that I'm going to play.

PJ. I knew that you could, but when we beat your butt, we'll still be friends, understood?

DI. What makes you think that you all will win?

PJ. Look, I just want you to know that we will still be friends.

DI. The way you sound, you think we're just going to roll over and die.

PJ. No, I know that you all will do your best. You will try. Hey, we should not get worked up over some little game. When it's over, we will still be the same.

There was silence on the other end of the phone. PJ was soon expecting to hear a tone.

DI. Yeah, we've been friends too long, and our friendship is too strong.

PJ. I thought for a minute that you were getting mad. You just don't know how those words make me feel. I'm so glad.

DI. I just want you to feel the same when we kick y'all's butt and win the game.

PJ knew that if they were to remain friends, the conversation would have to change; so he asked, "The girl I saw you with, what is her name?"

DI. Man, how did you see me with that girl? Anyway, her name is Cheryl.

PJ. I know that girl. She lives near. She is also very active. Doesn't she cheer?

DI didn't answer; instead, he asked, "After high school, what are your plans? I think I'll go into the army and become a man."

PJ. Well, I'm expecting to have a scholarship or two. I have plans to go to college. That's what I plan to do.

The game came, and PJ and his team did win. And at the end, they still were friends.

Graduation day was coming really soon. PJ's was at the end of May, and DI's was the first of June.

The day arrived, and as DI was watching PJ walk across the stage, it suddenly hit him that they had become of age. DI knew that PJ would probably go to college on a scholarship, but he also knew that he wouldn't be able to take the same trip. DI stood in the audience, and no matter how hard he would try, he couldn't stop a tear from falling from his eye.

The next day, bright and early, DI was in PJ's room; he knew that PJ would be getting up pretty soon.

PJ woke up, and he wasn't even surprised; he was used to DI coming over before he could open his eyes.

DI. Good morning, my friend. How does it feel? You're out of high school now. Does it even feel real?

PJ. Man, what are you talking about? You're about to do the same thing, and then you'll know how much joy it'll bring.

DI. Hey, I'm so happy for you signing that letter of intent, and I appreciate you inviting me to your big event.

PJ. Man, what are you talking about? It would be like a sin if I didn't invite my very best friend. You have only a few days before you'll be walking across that stage. Have you decided what you're going to do or where you're going to go? You do realize that it's kind of important, you know?

DI. Yeah, I spoke with the recruiter, and the army is for me. The navy tried to get me, but it's too much water for me to see.

PJ, I'm going to miss you, man. What are we going to do? When most people saw one, they saw two.

PJ. DI, stop talking like we're about to die. We can always get together if we try.

David's Dream

When David went into his room to go to sleep, he listened to his heart as it sped up its beat.

David would close his eyes, and he would start to dream. At first, it would be dreams of peace; so it would seem. Soon, he saw himself fighting in many wars, but so what? There was no one keeping any scores.

David laid in the bed wide awake, but he refused to get the medicine that he was supposed to take. All over his body, he begins to sweat; he sweated so much he got the whole bed wet. This would go on for days, sometimes even for weeks; it often felt like in his mind, someone was trying to speak.

He would then see images in his room; he quietly wondered, was he doomed? He would close his eyes, and he saw angels floating around; he then thought that if he had died, at least he was heaven bound. David thought that he would get up, resting for only about two hours; then he decided to get refreshed, and he got into the shower.

As he was in the shower, he felt a hand; he first thought that it was his wife, who might have gotten up and was playing, but then when he turned around, there was no one found.

Let me tell you a little about David when he was but a child. Let's just say he didn't have a behavior problem; he was just a little wild. Once, he was jumping over a ditch; his mother told him to stop. He fell in, and then she got a switch. The bus came, and he still had to go to school. But underneath his breath, he silently called her a fool. That day at school, it felt so long because he knew that he still, at the end of the day, had to go home.

David always had some really deep dreams, but he never gave too much thought about what they might mean. He wasn't like most of his friends, yet he would stand by them until the end.

Now, back in the shower, David still felt this hand, and then he heard a voice saying,

"You are definitely part of my plan. I have a job for you to do, a job that is pure, a job that is true. You might lose some friends and even some family, but in the end, it will be worth it. You will see."

With tears streaming down his face and snot running out of his nose, he asked, "What are the things that I'm to do? What do you suppose?"

Funny, David didn't hear another sound, but he felt like he was about to drown. Not drowning in the water, that wasn't it, but he felt like he was drowning in the Holy Spirit. David still thought to himself, *This just can't be for real. I've done some of everything except, to beg, borrow, and steal.*

David soon made his way out of the shower; it seemed as if he had been in there for hours. He dried off and went back into his room; he thought that the hour had come for them to be getting up soon.

His wife asked, "Why did you get up and take a shower when it's only two?" David said, "You might think that this is funny, but the Lord has something for me to do."

Daylight came, and David still felt the same. He thought that his life would be different; he thought that things would be magnificent. He still had to get up and cook breakfast; he still had to pick though the fruit that wasn't the freshest.

He thought to himself, *Lord, I thought you said that you were going to use me. I guess it's in your timing. I guess I have to wait and see.*

Days, weeks, and months went by; and things still felt the same. David began to wonder, *Did I do something wrong? Am I to blame?*

David gave no thought to his everyday life, how he always ministered to his children, how he ministered to his wife. He never thought about the people whom he met on the streets, how he was always friendly to everyone whom he would meet. How he would change an environment that might had been hostile, he did all of this simply with just his smile.

No, David thought that he was supposed to take the grand stand; he thought that he was supposed to be like a drum major up in front, leading the band.

One night, David got down on his knees; he started praying to the Lord. He wanted to know if he had done something wrong; he wanted to see. It seemed like he prayed all night without a reply; he really wanted to ask the Lord one simple question, "Why?"

He stayed on his knees so long that he would fall asleep; then and only then did the Lord start to speak.

"David, you're doing everything that you're supposed to do. You're staying within my words. You're staying true. I never said that you've been called to preach, yet you still spread my word to everyone you were supposed to reach. Too many of my people think that they should be behind closed doors, and they never get to the heart. They never get to the core. Just because I don't place you in front of a congregation, it doesn't mean that you won't be able to affect the whole nation. The people whom you come across and you talk and minister to, you might never know what I've called them to do. Just because some are known all over the world, and they have a name, it doesn't mean that at the end I'll know them. It doesn't mean those will be the ones I'll claim."

David woke up with peace in his heart. He was ready for a new day; he was ready for the new start.

Vanity

Carl was a man who liked to look into the mirror at himself. He didn't care too much about others; he didn't think that he needed anyone else. He had a nice body, and he had good looks; in his mind, he thought that was all that it took. Oh, he had family in his life, but he had a lot of women; he said that he didn't need a wife.

Carl thought of only things that he wanted to get; all of the other people in his life he didn't give a sh——. Some would say that he was awful selfish. Deep down inside, it was like he had a death wish.

He would go to the gym and pump a lot of weights, and when he got hungry, he just made sure that he had food on his plate. Carl had a good job, and he made decent money. But when it came to helping or giving to others, he would laugh; he thought that it was funny.

He didn't care that one day he would grow old and that looks could fade. He thought that he could always keep it up; it didn't matter, his age. Carl thought that young he would always stay; he used a lot of people who came his way.

Carl wouldn't listen to any advice that people tried to give. Carl simply thought, *This is my life, and I'm going to live.* The advice his mother tried to give, he thought that she didn't have a clue. Carl thought, *This is my life. I'm going to do what I want to do.* Carl went on with his life doing his own thing, never thinking about any results that his decisions might later bring.

Let's not forget, Carl was a good-looking young man and had a nice physical body. He had his pick of the ladies; he had a lot of hotties. He had one young lady whom he dated who went really crazy about him. She wasn't no bottom of the barrel; she was a gem. He soon grew tired of her and wanted to sow his wild oats; what he didn't know was that sowing those wild oats would soon make him choke.

Carl saw this other young lady; she was all that he really wanted. She had a body for days, a body that made Carl want to play. Carl thought, *This is the girl for me. I can get with her and how sweet things will be.* So Carl would just simply let his gem walk out the door; he thought, *Never again will I cross that floor.*

Carl soon got with the hottie with the nice body, and for a while, everything was really fine. But Carl soon saw another young lady, and he started to play with his hottie's mind. One day, Carl's hottie saw him out with another girl, and this was the time that turn Carl's world. She did things that caused Carl to lose it. Carl lost his head; he didn't give a sh—.

Needless to say that Carl went to jail; he had to humble down and call his mom for his bail. Carl injured his hand; things were never the same. His physique was no longer outstanding; it was just plain. It was like something happened deep down in Carl's brain. Carl had just become a regular guy. It was like he had just given up; he no longer would try.

Now, the gem that Carl had let walk out of his life, she was doing very well, and she still was no one's wife. One day, while Carl was walking down the street, he had lost his car; his old gem saw him walking from afar. She asked, "Why are you walking? Do you want a ride?" Carl held his head down to the ground and got inside.

She asked Carl how has he been; he replied, "Oh, not too good. Could you take me to the store so I can get a bottle of gin?" She replied, "Carl you never used to drink. What has happened to you? Is it to the bottom you're trying to sink?" What she would say, Carl truly heard. He listened to what she was saying; he listened to every word. Carl did not know how to reply. Carl felt like he would just rather crawl up and die.

She did not try to rub anything in, nor did she try to make him feel bad. But deep down in Carl's heart, he was really sad. He was sad about the way that he had treated her and how he had just lived his life in such a blur.

Carl told her, "I thought that it was all about me, the way I was built, the money I made, the girls I could get. I was living in vanity. I never really cared about others, even those who really cared for me. Where was my sanity? I pushed people away. I thought that life was just my game. I set the rule, and I decide how to play. Now I truly see that life is not just about me."

Some Life Stories: Stories within Stories

If everyone were to sit down and write their own life story, what would it tell? Maybe it would be about the people they thought they loved, the people whom they thought they knew so well. Maybe it will consist of the places they've been or some of the things that they have seen, or will it be just a blank canvas, just like a big blank screen?

People have many stories to tell, some they barely know and some they know too well.

Jim

Let's talk about Jim. Jim is a guy who is often in and out of jail, but he knows that his mother loves him so much that she will quickly make his bail. One day, Jim's mother passed away; and Jim knew that if he went back to jail, there he would have to stay.

Jim wasn't the one to work a steady job, but Jim likes to have fun. So Jim decided to do what he does, and that is to be a con. Jim thought of an easy way that he could get some money. Jim thought long and hard, and then he smiled; he thought of something that might be funny.

One day, Jim decided to pick up the Bible, not that he believed; but in his mind, he knew that people were so easy to deceive. Jim thought, *I can tell the people exactly what they want to hear. Then they will follow me. Just like you drive a car, they will go where I steer.*

Jim soon ran into some people he knew who thought the same way. Jim told them, "If we say what the people want to hear, they will be willing to pay." Jim and his friends soon started to get lots of money until it flowed out of their pockets, but Jim wasn't too happy; this wasn't it.

Nights came where Jim wasn't able to sleep at all. Jim would often have dreams where he would hear his name called. Jim would jump up, pouring with sweat; this is one con that Jim was starting to regret. At first, Jim didn't know what to do. But then he started reading, and he thought, *So your words are true?* Now the words that Jim reads, he truly believes; he no longer practices to deceive.

Faye

We now turn our attention to Faye. Faye was in her senior year of high school, and she was asked, after high school, what direction she would go. Faye thought for a while and then happily said, "Oh, I know." Faye said, "When I get out, I'll have a baby or three. Then I won't have to work, and the government will have to take care of me."

When Faye got out, she did just what she said, but her first baby was born dead. Faye's mind and her body were never the same; she started to realize that living life was no game. At this time, Faye didn't have another plan; then one day, Faye met this man. Faye thought, *I will get with him, and he will take care of me.* But things didn't work out that way; you will see.

Faye got with that man; at first, he treated her real good, but this man was straight from out the hood. After he got all of the sex that he wanted from Faye, he told her, "Hey, you have work and bring some money in. That's if you want to stay." Faye never prepared herself for any type of job, but the man told her, "You're good in bed, and you know how to slob."

Faye thought, *I'll just walk away from him. I'll just quit.* But then on the glass pipe, she quickly took another hit. Now, the man put Faye out to work the streets, but the money that she would make, she could not even keep. Soon, Faye would own nothing but the clothes that she had on her back, and she would sell those if it would get her another hit of crack.

Faye had a family that she would long to see, but she thought to herself, *I doubt if they would even recognize me.* Then one day, Faye met this other man, and she thought that she would switch; the other day, they found Faye's body lying in a ditch.

Joe

Joe was a young man; he could do no wrong. He was very positive; he was very strong. Joe found the Lord at a very young age. He knew the Bible very well; he knew every page. At a young age, Joe would recite "I Have a Dream" although he didn't have a clue of what those words would truly mean.

Joe's parents would often say, "Joe, you're called to preach." So Joe ate those words, and he decided to share the word to everyone he could reach. Joe's mother called him her little preacher man. She even thought his life out for him; she had it all planned.

Joe made it through elementary, middle, and junior high school without any problems; he followed all of the rules. Then one day, Joe met this girl named Jean. She was just the type of girl Joe needed; so it would seem. She went to Joe's house to meet his parents and to eat. Joe's mom and dad thought that she was so sweet.

One day, Jean looked into Joe's eyes with such a glance, and then she grabbed Joe's hand and slid it down into her pants. Joe's eyes got big, and his pants started to rise; the reaction Joe was having was much to his surprise.

You see Joe's mom and dad were so busy making plans for Joe, they forgot to teach him about other things that he should know.

Jean put her lips against Joe's, and she started to kiss. Joe's mind started to wonder, *What else in life have I missed?* Jean looked at Joe and asked, "Is this your first time getting with a girl? If so, Joe, I'm going to rock your world." Joe looked at her, and he had no clue. Joe didn't know what she was about to do. When it was all over, Joe felt good; he said, "I like to do it again if you would."

Joe made it back home, and he just wasn't the same. Joe's parents just knew that it was Jean to blame. Joe's dad took Joe to the side and said, "Come on, son. Let's go for a walk." While they walked, Joe's dad started to talk.

"Son, your mother and I made plans for your life, but we forgot to tell you things that you have to discover, and maybe one day, you might get a wife. I can tell by that big smile on your face that Jean has cut some corners. She has stopped the chase. Joe, when you're finished, it might seem like it was a lot of fun, but with it can come a lot of responsibility when it's all said and done. I should have taught you about the birds and bees and about making a baby. Yes, those things can happen when you get with a lady."

Joe looked at his dad; he didn't know what to say. He just kept walking while looking the other way. Joe heard what his dad had to say, but his mind was on getting with Jean another day.

True enough, Joe did make a baby with Jean, and later, they did get married. And they're happy; so it would seem. Joe never became this great preacher, but he did become a very good teacher.

Parents, do not label your children; let them run and play because young they will not always stay.

Jill

Jill was another young lady; she was fine as an expensive bottle of vintage wine. Jill had some beautiful, thick, but shapely legs; her legs would make most men stand up and beg. Jill had it all worked out; she had a plan. She thought that she would just get her a sugar daddy, you know, one who had expensive cars or a large SUV, something like a caddy. Jill wanted a man who had a wife because she still wanted to have her own life. Jill thought that a married man wouldn't be too hard to please; she thought all she would have to do was to rub on him and to tease.

Jill would go around with shorts on that had her cheeks hanging out, and her too small top, she would walk around watching all of the men mouth's drop. Jill spotted this guy; he was probably in his late forties or early fifties. She looked and at his finger; there was a ring, so she thought, *He must be married. So it would seem.* What Jill didn't know was, yes, indeed, that man did have a wife; but the events that she was about to go through would forever change her life.

Jill did all she could to get the attention of the man; she walked by him and touched his hand. The man looked at his wife and said, "This is the one. I bet with her we could have all kinds of fun." The wife left the man's side and went into a store. She didn't go deep inside; she just went inside the door.

Jill approached the man and said, "Hi, my name is Jill. I love so much if we could get together and watch television and chill. There are a lot of things that I would like to do to you, but by the way, I like nice things too."

The man replied, "I am married as you can see, but maybe we can come to some type arrangement. That's if you will agree."

Jill quickly rubbed her hand down the front of his pants; then the man looked at her backside with more than a glance. Jill said, "You like what you're looking at. This I can see, and I can tell that you will be a good fit for me. First there are a few things that I want you to know. You must always call me before you show. I have a certain amount of bills that I want you to pay. This must be done before our first lay, and most of all, I do like nice things, and looking at your wife, you do know how to give. So it would seem." Jill again backed up to the front of his pants, and then she did a slight move; she did somewhat of a dance. Jill thought to herself, *I will soon be living without a care.* But what she didn't know was that her life was soon to become a living nightmare.

The man then spoke, "Coming to your house is way too soon. How about me getting us a very nice hotel room? How about calling my phone so that I can have your number, and our deal will be set in stone?"

Jill said, "Wait a minute. What are you going to do for me? You have to do something to show me that you're for real so that I can see." Into her hand, he slipped three hundred dollar bills. That was enough for a start; that was enough for Jill.

The man asked, "Now how about me getting us a room, let's say tomorrow? How about around noon?" Then all of a sudden, the man's wife started to appear. Jill got a little closer; she was always near. She then placed a piece of paper in his hand; it had her number on it and read "call me as soon as you can."

The woman came out, and Jill walked away. She asked, "Who was that? I can leave if you want her to stay." The man just smiled and looked the other way.

The man was soon all alone, and he quickly called Jill up on her phone. "This is Jill. How can I help you?" The man spoke, "I was hoping that you remembered me from the mall. You gave me this piece of paper, and you asked me to call. I remember you after you put what you put into my hand. How can I forget? What is the plan?"

The man spoke with a very deep but soft voice, "Hey, whatever hotel you want to meet in, it's your choice." In Jill's mind, dollar signs flashed before her eyes, and then she thought about the new high rise. She told him about where she wanted to meet, and then she replied, "Since this will be our first get–together, you might not get all that you seek."

The man said with a suspicious tone, "Oh, I just want to lay with you. I can't wait to get you all alone."

The next day came, and for Jill, it was just a little too soon. But then she got a text telling her where and what room. Jill thought, *Do*

I really want to go? But I took his money. Can I really say no? Jill thought that she had a plan to just string him along, and after about an hour or two, she would simply just go home.

When Jill made it to the room, the lights were turned down low, and he even had rose petals placed on the floor. He had champagne poured in her glass. Jill thought to herself, *Wow, he is moving fast.* Jill then made a tremendous mistake; she drank the champagne and ate the chocolate strawberries off of the plate. Jill started to get light in her head; then she found herself lying naked on the bed.

The man's wife then came in, and from that moment on, Jill's nightmare would begin. They strapped Jill to the bed, and she looked like she was dead. They shot her up with cocaine; things in Jill's life would never be the same. The man and woman did everything that they wanted to do; they even invited a friend over, and he did things too.

When all were finished, they took Jill away, and now with them she will always stay. Jill has no more dreams and no more hope because now all she does is to stay high on dope.

Oh, Shelia

There once was this young girl named Shelia; it would have been your pleasure to meet her. Shelia had such a beautiful smile; some would say that you could see her smile for at least a mile. Shelia would smile at everyone she would meet. Shelia was friendly; she loved to speak. Shelia would often smile and say hello; it didn't matter if it was a female or a fellow.

One day, this old lady pulled Shelia to the side; she told Shelia, "Sometimes, your smile you might want to hide. You can't show your teeth to every man you meet. Oh, you still can speak. Some old men they are kind of funny. You show your teeth, and they think they can get your honey."

At first, Shelia didn't understand. Shelia questioned, *Why would this old lady put on her such a demand?*

As Shelia grew to be a beautiful teenager, nature was very kind to her. Shelia had lovely black hair; she made a lot of girls jealous, and got a lot of boys to stare. Shelia had a figure that was out of this world. Shelia was very sexy for a young teenage girl.

Yet Shelia was still Shelia; she would still walk around with her smile. Shelia didn't give in to her looks; she didn't even care about the styles.

This same old lady pulled Shelia to the side; she again told Shelia, "Baby, sometimes that smile you are going to have to hide. You can't show your teeth to every man you meet, and now that you're older, you should even watch just how you speak. Some of these old men are funny. They think that a smile means that they can get your honey."

Still, Shelia left and went about her way. Shelia didn't pay too much attention. Shelia just wanted to play.

Shelia was walking down the old freshly graveled street; a man was walking in the opposite direction, but they would meet. Shelia thought nothing of it. Shelia smiled and said hello; the old man smiled back and winked. Shelia thought that the wink was strange, which started her to think. The man turned around and started to walk with Shelia; he said, "I smiled at you, and you smiled at me too. Is there something on your mind? Is there something that you want to do?" He tried to put his arm over Shelia's shoulder; he said that it would be nice if he could get to hold her.

Just as they were walking by, this same little old lady yelled, "Leave that young girl alone before I bust your eye."

Shelia ran to the old lady. The old lady asked, "You showed your teeth to him, didn't you, baby? Baby, there are so many things in this old world, and right now they might not make sense to a young teenage girl."

From that moment on, with that old lady, Shelia would go sit and talk. Shelia watched whom she smiled at, and she watched where she would walk. Shelia grew up to be a very respectful, fine young lady; she made it through high school and college without any babies. Even today, Shelia still has that beautiful smile; and yes, they still say that you can see it for miles. And she still remembers what the old lady used to say even though she has long passed away. "You can't show your teeth to every man that you meet, but it's still okay for you just to speak."

Stanley

There once was this guy; he was very handsome, yet he was very shy. This young man's name was Stanley.

Stanley was so shy that when he talked with others, he couldn't look them in their eye. With Stanley, all the other kids used to pick; some would push him around, and some would hit him with sticks.

Stanley would often go home with tears in his eye; he wanted to fight back, but he was just too shy.

In school, Stanley was as smart as a whip; through all of his classwork, he would just zip. Yet Stanley still didn't have any friends; with other kids, he just didn't blend in. Stanley would sit by himself and eat his lunch while the other students would just bunch. One day, this new girl came to the school; she didn't know or care too much for the "stay away from Stanley" rule.

Stanley had finally met a friend, and it was no way that he wanted this to end. Stanley would make himself smile, but for him to do this, it did indeed take a while. The young girl didn't mind because she loved to talk; she would even hold Stanley's hand while they walked.

Stanley became brave enough to hold her hand. Stanley was finally developing into a brave young man. Stanley would now hold conversations; he even talks about having relations. Yes, indeed, Stanley talked about planting his seed.

Then came graduation day; once again, it was hard for Stanley to find words to say. The young girl said, "Stanley, I know that things might not be the same after today."

Once again, Stanley felt the sadness in his heart; he thought, *How could this be? I have to get a fresh start.* Stanley told her, "I'm going to college, but I'm taking a double load. I can graduate in two years. This I was told. Then I'd go and get my master's and PhD. It won't take too long. You will see. I'm going to make a lot of money." But the other guys were listening, and they thought that this was funny.

After graduation, they all went their separate ways, and Stanley did exactly what he said he would do with great pay. Now the guys who used to make fun of him come and ask for jobs. They come in crawling; some even sob.

Oh, the young girl did wait. Stanley and she got married, and a couple of babies they did make.

Spencer

Spencer thought that he had a true friend, you know, one whom he could count on again and again.

Spencer felt through the storms, through the rain; he felt so much hurt, so much pain. He thought, *When will this hurt and pain end?* He tried so hard to turn to his friend. He thought he was the one whom he needed to see. But it turned out, Spencer thought, *He would just turn his back on me.* He thought for sure that he was his friend. But then he was told that he was no good, and he was the reason that Spencer's freedom was sold. He told the man that he did the crime, and now Spencer is the one locked up doing his time. Spencer thought in his mind, *Not my homeboy. He just tossed me away as if I was a used-up toy.* For now, Spencer just sits behind these iron bars while he's out riding around in his fancy cars. Spencer thought there will be a day that he will get out, and then he will make him pay, that he will make him scream and shout. Now Spencer sits here with so much hate; at night, when he lies down and tries to sleep, it is his manhood that they take. At first, Spencer tried to scream; he tried to fight. But sooner or later, there was not any light. When Spencer opened his eyes, he saw the doctor; he saw the nurse. He then opened his mouth, and he started to curse. He thought, *How could this have happened to me? Why couldn't I have opened my eyes? Why couldn't I see? I should have listened when I was told to stay away from him, that he has a very bad soul. But I thought that I knew it all, and now he became the reason that I would fall.* All of a sudden, a light comes on. Spencer wasn't in the prison; he was at home. Was this a vision or something that he would wake up to see, or was it simply a warning that was meant to be?

Today, when his homeboy called, he asked Spencer to go with him, with him to the mall. Spencer thought about all of the hurt and pain; he thought about the storms and all the rain. Spencer told his homeboy that he wasn't going to go; his homeboy got mad, but Spencer still said no. His went anyway, and he tried to rob a jewelry store. But he got caught before he made it to the door. His homeboy tried to tell them that it was not his plan; he told them that Spencer was the one, that he was the man.

Spencer was at home, not even dressed; then he heard a hard knock on his door, and he became stressed. The police came in, and they asked him if he knew his friend. Spencer said yes, but our friendship had come to an end. He told them that he got mad today when he called; he said that he had turned him down. "I didn't go with him to the mall." They asked Spencer if he knew what he was going to do. He told them no, that he didn't know; he didn't have a clue. Spencer asked them, "By the way, where is he?" They told Spencer that he was in jail, waiting to see if there will be any bail.

The police officer told Spencer, "You all think that your so-called friend you'll have all of life until one turns around and stabs you in your back with a knife."

Spencer's eyes were finally opened, and now he could see. "Wait a minute. Did he try to blame this crime that he did on me?"

The officer told Spencer, "Don't try to get even, and don't walk around mad because you don't have the friend that you thought you had. I guess now your eyes are opened, and you say never again. You say that you will never call just anyone a friend."

Tony's Thoughts

Tony was a man whom most people would trust, but what they didn't know was that Tony was a man who had a humongous problem with his thoughts of lust.

Tony prayed each and every day; he prayed that those thoughts of lust would be taken away. Tony would often read the great book. But a thought of lust would appear, and then he would again be hooked.

Tony would often shake his head to remove those thoughts, but then Tony would wonder if those thoughts were all of his fault. It was like visions of lust just danced in Tony's head; he thought that the visions would be there even when he's dead.

Tony would often plea; he would often beg, "Lord, please take these thoughts of lust out of my head."

Tony longed for a vision of beauty and peace; he often hoped to see, he often hoped that the thoughts of lust would soon flee.

One day, Tony had a thought; what if he didn't have any eyes? But then he remembered that the thoughts that he was having came from deep down inside.

Once again, Tony would read; he would plea, "My Lord, please take these lustful thoughts away from me."

Tony asked how he could have a pure heart, how he could get a fresh start.

Over the years, Tony lived a very precarious life; he had done different things to different women, but none of them would be his wife. While Tony was doing these things, he thought, what's the harm? He said all he was doing was filling them with a lot of his charm.

Tony often thought that the feelings that he was having he could really trust, but he had no idea that those were the feelings that he was running from, the feelings of just lust.

One day, in Tony's heart, a light started to shine; all of the things he was doing he had to learn to leave them behind.

Tony no longer walks in those same steps. He has turned over a new leaf; he now stands on a new belief. And now the thoughts that Tony once had that were filled with nothing but lust, they are now thoughts of joy and peace, thoughts that he can trust.

One Long Day

Roy is someone who others never wanted to get to know, he's the type that would get up before the rooster would crow.

One long day, while Roy was just waiting for time to pass, he watched a little bunny just sitting in the grass. But where he was, it started to get really hot, so he decided to move into a shadier spot.

While he was sitting underneath a tree, he was then chased by a small little honeybee. He began to scream; he began to yell. He started to run, and then he fell. He falls in the grass, and his pants got a stain. But he soon forgot about the stain when he felt the pain.

At first, he didn't notice; it was hard to feel. But then he looked down and saw the bottom of his heel. It was a lucky thing that Roy was standing outside because he screamed so loud, one would have thought that someone had died.

Roy's neighbor came outside, and he took one look. Roy thought that his ankle was broken, but it turned out, his shoe just came off of his foot.

Roy thought that he would go into his home and stay, but when he went inside, he saw that his dog had run away. Roy thought, *How could this be? Can anything else possibly happen to me?*

Well, Roy said, "I know, I will cook me something to eat." But when he opened his fridge, all he had were two little chicken feet.

Roy decided to get into his car and go buy himself some groceries, but then he remembered that there was not any store locally. Roy took one look at his gas hand, and then he thought, *I should have put some gas in my car, oh man!*

Yeah, Roy wasn't having a very good day, but it didn't detour him at all; he just continued anyway.

On his way to get some gas, his vehicle started to quit; he then thought, *Man, I'm not going to get there if I don't get there awful quick.* Roy got out of his car to get his gas can out of his trunk only after he had dug through all of the other junk.

Roy started walking, and he made it to the station. He thought it seemed like a week. He was pumping his gas, but then his can started to leak. Roy threw his hands in the air and screamed, "Why? I can't beat you, so why do I try?"

Then this nice lady pulled into the next stall; she asked, "Do you need any help, any help at all?"

Roy, with a smile on his face, said, "Could you help me get back to my place?"

She answered, "I sure can, and by the way, you're a very handsome man."

Roy soon thought, *Today might not be so bad. Things happen in your life that might seem to get you down, but at the end of the day, they just might make you glad.*

Tim

When Tim was young, he had such a beautiful girl. She was his best friend; she was his world. They used to get up early in the morning and play; they made the most of every single day.

Tim laughed and talked with her as if she could understand; he even told her of his life plans. He taught her how to sit, to come, and to stay; yes, they were best friends until one horrific day.

The day started off like many, so many, of the rest. Tim brushed his teeth, washed his face, and then got dressed. He then grabbed his friend, and they went outside. His mother then went to the store; she asked Tim if he wanted to ride. Tim decided that he would stay because outside with his friend, he wanted to play.

Time went by, and Tim decided to go inside for a quick bite. He left his friend outside; he thought that she would be alright. Tim suddenly heard a car as if it had jammed it's brakes; he then wondered if leaving his friend outside was a mistake.

Tim quickly dropped his sandwich, and he ran outside. But it was too late; his best friend had died. Tim reached down, picked her up, and held her in his arms; it was extremely sad because the car, he had heard, was his mom's.

Tim's mom stood there with tears in her eyes; she didn't know what to say, so she didn't even try. After a while, she told Tim, "You have to be brave. We can bury her in the backyard. We can mark her grave."

With tears still in his eyes, Tim looked at his mom, "I know that you didn't mean to cause her any harm, but can you tell me how this came to be? Was she sitting in the driveway, or did you just not see?" His mom told him, "Yes, I could see, but your little friend just ran in front of me."

Tim carried her to the backyard to dig her grave; he even made a headstone so that the spot could forever be saved.

A few weeks went by. Tim's mom asked, "Do you want another friend? Do you want to try?" Tim looked at his mom and said, "Maybe some other day. I'm still not over my best friend passing away."

At first thought, Tim's mom was about to pick up her coffee mug; but instead, she turned around and gave Tim a big hug. Tim looked up and her, and he had a very large smile. "Mom, I guess I've been needing this hug for a very long while."

Tim said, "I lost my friend, which is true, but the best friend that I could have is standing right here with me, which is you."

The Crying Soul

When you sit in a dark and dying space, there can't be any laughter nor a smile upon your face.

Richard was a quiet and misguided little man; when he was young, the only game he played was kick the can. Richard would retreat into a cold, dark, and gloomy room, not to come back out anytime too soon.

His mother would ask, "Richard, why don't you go out and make some friends? But when he did, he would just run away from them in the end. Richard once had a pretty little dog; he called her Clyde. But Clyde didn't live too long; for some unknown reason, she just died.

Once Richard tried to put a smile on his face, it was a smile of emptiness; it was a smile of disgrace. Richard's uncle once tried to teach Richard how to fish; his uncle said it was as if Richard had some type of death wish. He told Richard's mom that she should get Richard some help, but she said that Richard was just being a normal little boy; so she felt.

Richard started to grow; he became a teenager. Then his mother had different feelings; she felt that her life was in danger. Richard would sit with this dark and gruesome grin on his face; one could tell what was on his mind, and it was all sin. Richard's mother had become very afraid; she tried to hide all of the weapons, down to the smallest blade.

One day, Richard opened his mouth, and he began to speak; this was unusual because he hadn't mumbled a word for several weeks. Richard told his mother, "I would like to get me a gun. I want to start hunting. I think it would be lots of fun."

Richard's mother didn't know what to say nor if his words were true; she really didn't know what to do. She never asked Richard what was he planning to hunt; she was really afraid, just to be blunt.

Richard's mother, being afraid, ordered him a rifle and the ammunition; she told Richard that she would give it to him under one condition.

Richard quickly snatched the rifle and the ammunition out of her hands; he growled, *"You don't give me any conditions, woman!"*

The rifle Richard started to load, and then he pointed it at the neighbor's house that was across the road. Richard's mother grabbed the rifle's barrel and pulled it down; the rifle went off, and then there was no sound. Richard thought that he had shot a hole through the door, but then he saw his mother lying in a pool of blood on the living room floor.

Richard shouted, *"Look what you made me do. You're to blame."* But then Richard continued on as if everything was the same. He never got his mother up, out of the pool of blood. He never felt any remorse; he never felt any love.

Bright and early the next day, Richard was camouflaged down; he went outside and shot the first person that he found.

Richard thought, *This wasn't any fun. Killing one at a time is such a bore. I know what I'll do. I'll take my rifle with me into the store.*

Richard walked into the store, and he started to shoot. There were people falling and screaming, but for Richard, there was no sound. But he did manage to laugh as he saw the people falling to the ground.

Now we come back to Richard, sitting inside of his tiny cell; he often wonders, *Is there truly a physical place called hell?* In his heart he's unable to feel any remorse; he feels like this is the hand in life that he was given and that he didn't have much of a choice. He sits here on death row, never cracking a smile, waiting on the day that he'll walk his last mile.

The Thrill Is Gone

What is one to say when it appears as if the thrill has gone away? Yet we try to live on, pretending that our feelings for each are still strong.

Earlier in our lives, we had a child or two, but now we hardly ever do the things that we once loved to do. We're just like a balloon that has lost its air; the body is still there, but for some reason, we just don't care.

We often leave the house, you going your way and me going mine; but at the end of the day, we come back together, pretending that everything is fine.

We hardly touch each other and play, you know the thing that would make us want to stay. You walk through the house not saying a kind word; if a mouse would fart, that sound would be heard. When I try to hold and touch you, you pull away; you act like I'm some strange dog off the streets, a complete stray.

When we took those vows as husband and wife and we said that "I do," I thought that the love that we had for each other would always be true.

Yes, over the years, we have had some laughs, this we know; but now you only want me on your arm when you're trying to put on a show. When we go around your friends, it's all smiles and grins; but deep in my heart, I'm asking, *Is this the end?* Yet once again when we get back home, it still feels like I'm all alone.

When I first met you, you never drank, gambled, or cursed. Is it because of me? Have I brought out your worst? When two come together, we're supposed to build each other up, but it appears to me that you're about to self-destruct. Now, I have to beg for you to hold me and to get a kiss. Did something happen along the way? Was there something that I missed?

I've done everything that I know to do, everything I could; if I could turn back the hands of time and start over, Lord knows that I would.

When we sit down and talk, you say that everything is fine; but if so, how come it feels like that you're not mine? I know that we're not the same as we were ten years ago, but since we should have grown together, shouldn't each other we still know? Time together should make our hearts strong, but does that mean our thrill should be gone?

I want to bring back how we used to laugh and play, those things that made me to always want to stay. I used to love to see that smile upon your face, that smile that made all of my blues to just erase. The way that you used to hold my hand, I want to get that feeling back if we can.

Now, I've done everything that I know to do, but if we are going to stay together, it does take two. When I mentioned the word "divorce," you say that's not the direction you want for you, that's not the course. So now you have me at a loss. I want to save what we have, but at what cost?

I have to admit that we still a few laughs and things, but those few laughs and things are too far in between.

Each night when I lie in bed, my heart wants to cry, but I refuse to let one tear drop fall from my eye. If there is someone else that you would rather be with, I wish you would tell me and tell me really quick. I'm not out in the streets mate shopping, and I won't be out there in different beds, just hopping.

You might look at me and think that I'm too old. But my body is still warm, and I'm not yet cold. I might not be the one who looks the best, but I want you to know that I can still compete with the rest. Just because my hair might have some gray, you might think that I have to depend on you, and here I have to stay.

A lot of my money I've spent on you because once again, I thought that our love was surely true.

Now you stand there telling me that if I leave, I would be truly missed; but while I'm here, I have to beg and plea with you for just a simple kiss. If there is a problem with you, I wish you would tell me because I'm here for you; can't you see? I know that over the years, things can go wrong, but this is another reason why our love should be strong.

I'm not going to beg, but there is one last thing that I want to say; if you truly like and love me, I'm willing to stay.

On the Warpath

Bill had a problem with going and staying asleep; some would say it was because of the food he would eat. Even when there were rain, lighting, and thunder, he would just lie there, and his mind would wander. He had so much on his mind; so it would seem. Some say that it was because of his dreams.

Bill used to be in his bed, and he would fight; he would just lie there and do it half of the night. Bill used to go to bed when it got really late; he even tried to get the right amount of food on his dinner plate. The doctors tried to give Bill different kinds of pills, but pills were against Bill's will.

One night, while Bill was lying in bed, he dreamed that he had shot the enemy in the head. Bill often had dreams of making a kill, but before he did, he would wake up instead. Bill used to tell the doctors, but they didn't seem to care. So his dreams continued until they turned into nightmares.

One night, while Bill was lying in bed, he would toss and turn; and then in his chest, he felt a sizzling burn. Bill thought, *The enemy has shot me. I must run. I must flee.* Bill started to kick his legs as if he was running away, but the he thought, *I'm a soldier. I must not run. I will stay.* Bill turned around and picked up his gun; he then started to return fire. He thought this is fun.

In the morning, when Bill awakens, he looked over at his wife. She was not breathing; he had taken her life. There were bullet holes all in his bedroom; there was a cold dark feeling, but it was the middle of June. Bill thought to himself, *How did this happen? The enemy came for me. I will get them back; this I guarantee.*

So Bill got up and dressed. He put on his combat boots. He loaded his guns. He went outside, and he started to shoot. He first shot the woman who was walking her dog; when the neighbors heard the shots, the police they did call. Bill looked at his neighbor's house that was next door; he shot it up, and they fell to the floor. He shot the dog as it began to bark; he even shot the sidewalk, and there was a spark.

In Bill's mind, he was back at war although there was no body count; there was no score. Bill just knew that he had to kill all that he could, and that he could do; he surely would. Bill would move like he was in combat, and that made it even harder for the police to track.

As the police would search for Bill, they covered the grounds, but everywhere they turned, another dead body would be found. Bill was no regular soldier; he wasn't just plain. Bill was a super soldier; he was well trained. Police in that town wondered when the killing will cease; and then all of a sudden, they found dead police.

While Bill was running, he tripped and hit his head; and then he looked around and thought, *Look at what I did.* Bill then threw his gun and ammunition down to the ground; the police soon came, and Bill they did surround. Bill got on his knees with his hands held high; he told the police, "You have me. Fighting you, I won't even try." They soon took Bill to jail, and there was no bail. Bill was locked up for the rest of his life, but there was only one person that he regretted killing, and that was his wife.

A Letter from My Friend

I can clearly understand how you feel, my friend. But let me assure you; this is only the beginning and not the end. I know that there are times when you might have a lot of doubt, but we all go through those moments that we might just want to pout. You must remember that it's more than just your life. It's me, your friend; your children; and your wife.

I know you feel like that you've done a lot in your life and you've carried a heavy load, but I can assure you that if you were to compare, it wasn't so heavy if the truth be told. The load that you thought you were carrying was not your load to bear because you and I both know that load was just a quarter of your share. It's just like that poem "Footprints in the Sand"; you can't carry life's full loads for you are just a simple man.

Life can so often throw you some curveballs, but that doesn't mean that you just give up and fall. Whether you're poor as hell or you win the lottery and strike it rich, it doesn't even matter if you're digging a ditch. You can be the talk of the town, or you could feel like you're about to drown. I guess what I'm trying to say is that we all can go through life's ups and downs.

You can find somewhere to go; you can simple run away. But one thing about it, there will definitely be somewhere that you will have to stay. And one day, you will wake up and look into that mirror. You will open your eyes, and then you'll see. You will have to say to yourself, "It doesn't matter where I go. There I will be."

My answer to your letter might have you somewhat confused, but I'm not going to let you just feel sorry for yourself; this I refuse. Just like your letter, you painted a picture on a blank canvas for me to see. I'm giving you an answer back to some degree. I want you to open your mind and start to think because the answers that I might give you, they might not smell good; in fact, they just might stink.

Yes, we do have to remember that we are the righteousness of God in Christ Jesus; but even while we're remembering that, we can feel like we want to cuss. You thought going through life would be just a breeze, but with each opportunity we encounter, we really need to seize. I know that our Lord has told us to just be still, but being still is us doing things within ourselves that are not of his will.

You asked me that since you won the lottery, would it be wrong for you not to share? I know you, and I know your heart; this would be extremely hard for you because you really care. I also know that you would not simply just give it away; you'll give some just enough to help to path another's way.

Negative thoughts will always cross your mind. We live in a negative world; those thoughts will find. We have people fighting for power, position, and money; and there are even those who think that this is truly funny. Our country, they have turned it into a joke; it's enough to make a sane person want to choke. I will not dwell on the negativity; let's instead reflect upon our productivity.

Over the years, we have grown into productive older men. We have encountered our ups and downs; we have even made it through some of our sins. Let me get one thing straight; we are still here, and that in itself should be enough for us to want to stand up and cheer. Look, there's a poem that I found that I think you should read. It's written by my friend, Paul; it's simply titled "Thank You."

Why couldn't I have seen you walking on the waters that were so deep?
Why couldn't I have seen you walking on the sea beneath your feet?
Why couldn't I have seen you making the waters so tranquil?
Why couldn't I have seen you making the winds to just be still?
Why couldn't I have seen you when you brought the dead back to life?
Why couldn't I have seen you when you did it not once but thrice?

Why couldn't I have seen you making the blind man to see?
Why couldn't I have seen you all the times that you've been there for me?
Why couldn't I have seen you every time when I would slip, trip, and fall?
Why couldn't I have seen you when you carried me through it all?
Why couldn't I have seen you every time I would break down and cry?
Why couldn't I have seen you when you dried every tear from my eye?
Why couldn't I have seen you all the times that I was stressed?
Why couldn't I have seen you when you helped me to be my best?
Why couldn't I have seen you when you made me part of your plan?
Why couldn't I have seen you when you helped me to grow into this man?
Lord, you have always been there for me.
And if I had just simply opened my heart, I would have been able to see.

Thank you.

Now, friend, as you can see, over the years, our Lord has been really good; and it didn't matter how we walked or how we stood. He brought us through our trials, dreams, and even our nightmares; and he did this to show us just how much he cares. Not because of the things that we've done, he wanted to show us how we should serve and not to only the ones who we think deserve. In us, he wants his message of love to grow because when it does, it's him that we truly begin to know.

My friend, I pray that this return letter has helped you out. I know it's one of those letters that might not make you want to scream and shout. I just want you to know that if ever you're feeling down, in him your joy can be found. Please do not hesitate to contact me again because brothers in Christ we will always be, and most of all, we will always be friends.

My Dearest

As I walk through this land of pain and sorrow, I can't help but wonder if you will be here for me again tomorrow. Your hopes and your dreams aren't very far, but they seem to have left many scars. You traveled down many dark and lonely roads, but you say that the things you've done were the things you were told.

Life can have its many ups and downs; some will keep you smiling, and some will bring you frowns. When you're by yourself, it can be dark and cold; it can be like going through life with many potholes. Just when you think that things are going smooth, you feel like you're hitting your stride, and you're hitting your groove, something pops its ugly head up and makes you think that you're about to lose.

My dearest, I've waited such a long time to hear you speak some words; but now that I hear them, I must say that I'm a bit disturbed. You say that before you found me, you had no life; but now that you have me, you're eaten up with strife. But when I say that I'm about to go, you hold me tight, and you just say no.

My past actions might have put some fear into your heart, but given another chance, we can get off to a fresh start. I know that I'm the one who chose to walk away, while all of the time, you were asking me to stay. What you didn't realize was that something in me had rolled up and died; it rolled up in my heart deep down inside. It was like I didn't know how to love; it was like I had never received any from up above.

The words that you are saying are probably true, yet your actions are so confusing. I really don't know what to do. It's like you're a different person every day. I don't know which one of you I want to stay. One of you is filled with passion and makes me feel alive while one of you just talks slang and is just full of jive. One of you is just so kind and sweet; you come in and sweep me off of my feet while one of you seems to be evil and mean, and all you want to do is to jump in between. Yes, you buy me presents and things, but when you're mean, you're awful mean.

I know you say that I can be sweet and kind; there's a lot going on in my mind. I know you say that I can be mean. But it's like there is a lot of people inside of me, and they're playing tag team. I never want to hurt you, yet I never want to let you go; there's a feeling deep inside me that I want you to know.

When I'm lying next to you, the cares of this world seem to shut off; but I can't help but wonder, *What in my life will this happiness cost?* Yes, when I'm lying with you, it feels so good; and yes, I would be here beside you all day if I could. Just when things seem to be going our way and just when I want to ask you to stay, a different side of you seem to come out, and then all you do is to fuss and shout. How can you expect me to live my life this way? How can you ever imagine that I would want to stay?

You know we were supposed to pass like two ships in the night, but it's now that I don't want to let you out of my sight. Your eyes are like a burning fire; they often ignite my deepest desire. And you know that the thought of you can warm my darkest nights. I just wish that it was enough to take away my biggest frights. You know and I know that this might not be, but who knows? Maybe, just maybe, we should wait and see.

The room is dark and cold when you're no longer young, and you're growing old. The storms come, and the winds blow; all you want is for the pain and the loneliness to go. The tides go out, and they come back in; all you want is that special friend. Just like in the early morning the sun shines, I just want someone that I can call mine.

I do understand the words that you speak, but I can't live my life not knowing which person I'll have from week to week. I do have a life, and I do want to live. And I do have a lot of love in me that I want to give. I go to bed; and I hold my pillow so tight because I want to know, for me, what is right. It's like a cloud that not only hovers over my bed, but it's like that cloud also hovers in my head.

It's like I can see the pain that's on your face, the pain that's in your heart; maybe one day, you will be ready for a fresh start. You must learn that I'm not that person who was just after lust, but you will not know until you learn again to trust. But until then, the winds will blow such a bitter cold. And then one day, you will wake up, and you'll be lonely and old.

My dearest.

Tomorrow

They say that when a person dies, a child is born; so in this world, which one should we truly mourn? New Life can be precious; new life can be nice. But given any thought, it should be thought about twice. This world is full of pain and sorrow; people are living like there is no tomorrow.

Jason was a nice-looking young man; his whole life, he liked to plan. He met a young lady, and they dated about four or five years. They went through hard times; they shed some tears. Then one day, Jason decided to make her a proper lady; they got married, and in about three years, she was having a baby.

After the baby came, things just weren't the same; and wouldn't you know, Jason decided to go. The baby grew; he was no longer small. As a matter of fact, he was pretty tall. He became an exceptional athlete, and he was really fast and quick on his feet. He stood about six feet four; and wouldn't you know, Jason tried to enter back into the door.

While the child was young, Jason acted as if he was a shame, but now he goes to all of his games. Jason sits in the stands, screaming and acting wild; he wants everyone to know that's his child. When the game is over, Jason is the first one down to the field. His son doesn't seem too happy; he doesn't seem to be thrilled.

Jason's son has excellent grades; if you look at his report card, he had all As. He's in the top ten of his class, which should make Jason happy, because he was almost dead last. It was his last year of school, and he was also a top ten recruit; he needed to have a really nice suit.

Jason went to this store called something bad. He brought his son a suit that looked like something that his grandfather had. Jason really thought that he was doing a great thing, but the suit started to come apart at the seams.

It was signing day, and his son had to choose. Jason thought, *Should I go?* He thought, *I have nothing to lose.* Jason showed up, and he looked at his ex-wife; he thought, *I wonder how it would have been if I had been there his whole life.* In Jason's mind, he was truly glad; but in his heart, he was really sad.

After Jason's son signed, he went to his friends and his mother, and he then went and picked up his little brother. Jason wanted to walk to him, but he thought, *What's the bother?* His son then turned and walked over to his stepfather.

Jason then turned and started to walk away, but he heard a familiar voice that called out hey. Jason's son walked over and said, "I'm glad that you came. Look, Dad, there is no fault. There is no blame. Mom told me that you two were really young. You got married, thinking that it would be fun. She said that the pressure of being a husband and a father was too much for you and that you did what you thought that you had to do. But you are my dad, and I still love you."

Jason turned and looked his son face to face; he said, "Son, I was young and foolish, and things happened that can't be erased. I'm just happy that you turned out to be a great young man, and if there is anything I can do for you, I'll do it if I can."

Jason's son gave him a hug and asked him to stay just when Jason was about to walk away. His stepfather came over and shook Jason's hand; he told him, "I'm glad to finally meet you. I've heard that you're a good man."

Jason told him, "I'm really happy to finally meet you, and all of the things that I've heard about you, I see for myself, are true. I guess I just want to say thank you."

Jake and Joan

THE HONEYMOON

Jake and Joan made it to their destination.

Their honeymoon night was oh so anticipated.

It was finally there, and they were so elated.

They made their way to the bedroom.

And it wasn't a moment too soon,

They began to take off their clothes.

But first, they made sure that the blinds were closed.

When Joan looked down and saw Jake's little man,

She thought to herself, *All of that in me, I guess I'll do what I can. I'll work with as much as I can. I'll do my best. I'll just have to use my hand and do whatever with the rest.*

Jake looked at her body; it was like a dream come true.

He thought, *Come on, Jake, be patient. You know what to do.*

He laid her gently on the bed.

And then inside he started inserting his head.

But just as soon as he was about to start, she grabbed his hand and held on tight, and thought, *This might take all night.*

She said, "I can't believe that I came first. That's not right. Jake, I held
back as long as I could.
"But Jake, my love, your little man feels really good.
"Now, come on, my big man, show me what you can really do
"Because as you can see, I'm ready for round two."

Jake was so happy that they had decided to wait.
And then she flipped him over like a pancake.
She got on top, and she started to ride.
She started to ride with every inch of him deep inside.
Both of them were pouring wet with sweat.
And then all of a sudden, Joan got Jake and the whole bed wet.
Jake laid there with his toes spread out wide
Because he just came deep down inside.
Joan looked at him with a smile on her face.
And then she said, "This is one memory that I'll never erase."
They both got up so they could change the sheets.
Jake wondered, *Is this a performance that I can repeat?*

He said to Joan, "Before we go to sleep, your body I want to see."
She laid there and said, "When we wake up, you had better be ready
for round three."

Both Jake and Joan knew that sex wasn't the only thing
Because they had become friends before the wedding rings.

As Jake laid there with Joan's head on his chest, thoughts danced
around in his head.
He tried to think about Cleo; he tried to think about the kids.

But it was like a block was placed in his mind, and there was no room to give.

And then he heard a voice, "Let the dead bury the dead. You shall live."

Just at that moment, Joan woke up and planted a sexy kiss on his lips, and they wanted it to last.

They took their time. They hugged and kissed. They didn't go very fast.

Jake hoped in his mind that this wasn't a dream

Because it felt too good; so it might seem.

Joan then started to make sounds; she started to moan.

Jake knew then that he was the man, and he had it going on.

He knew then that he could have gone all night.

He could have gone to the early morning light.

Joan thought, *This is truly my man.*

And I'm going to please him every way that I can.

She thought to herself, *If this is a dream, please don't wake me.*

If he's not right here beside me, I don't want to wake up to see.

When they were finished, they decided to take a shower.

The shower didn't last five or ten minutes; it lasted about an hour.

He looked into her eyes, and he saw a reflection of himself.

He knew in his heart that there could be no one else.

She was about to get out, but Jake closed the shower door.

Wow, can you believe it? It was time for round four.

The next morning came.

Finally, they decided to take a break; Jake was hungry. They decided to go out and take in the sights. It was their honeymoon. And they didn't pay all of that money to just stay in the room.

Saying Goodbye

As Jim, speaking of himself in third person, sat down and wrote a letter, knowing that he only had hours to live, he wondered if he had anything more to give.

He started to reflect back over his life; he thought about his kids, his ex-wife. He thought about some of the things that he had done, some in the name of lust, some in the name of fun. The lives that he might have touched, the lives that has meant so much.

Jim is a pretty good man; he has done several different things over his life span.

Jim thought that what he was about to do was fine; he didn't think that there were too many people that would mind. Jim didn't know that he was so loved, with the exception of the love from above. He knew that some would read this and try to judge.

Those of you who do try to judge him, Jim could only hope that you could look through his eyes so that you could see. Some will say that Jim was just angry at the world or that he was just hurt because he had just lost his girl.

Jim is a Christian, and he does believe in God. But even with his strong belief, things are really hard. He does believe that Jesus died and went into and rose from the pits of hell, and for this reason, from hell he needs no bail.

Some of you might think that his life has always been in shackles; no, that's not true, but it's just at this very moment he just doesn't know exactly what to do. He has had such a wonderful life although he's been married not only once but twice.

Jim might be thinking too far ahead; he's still thinking that he might be better off dead. He's thinking that if he flips his next page, things just might be worse. Jim still thinks that he is living underneath a curse.

He thought living his life and just being himself and not pretending or trying to be anyone else can be kind of hard, but once you give into that pressure, it is hard to discard. Jim lost his train of thought; he tries to get back on track. He thought this letter is just like his life; he doesn't know where he's at.

Jim thought that when he turned over and gave his life to Jesus, things would get easy, but it was then that things started to get out of control and often freaky. It was then that he discovered that he could not have a dime, and he still could make love to two women at a time. Jim thought he had to make better decisions because he saw his life heading toward a huge collision. His life was spending out of control. He thought, *How did it get like this?* No one really knows.

He thought about why he was saying goodbye. Was he just going to give up? Was he not willing to try?

Jim thought, *I have to figure out what I'm compelled to do.* He has to figure out what's the meaning, what is true. He thought he's lived his life off of wine, women, and lust. Is this his true meaning? Is this what he is to trust? Jim thought that he did things that most people haven't done, all because it made him feel good, and he thought it to be fun.

Jim thought saying goodbye wouldn't be so hard to do, but he had to find his meaning in life; he must find what is true.

Jim thought if you could see the world the way that he sees it, he wonders if you would want to continue, or would you want to quit? Often, he would think of the people that he would leave behind. Would they even care? Would they even mind? Jim wants to say to those who are left he is so sorry, that he is only thinking about himself. Jim knows that everyone's life time is ticking, and no one really has long, so he wants to advise everyone to try to keep living and try to be strong.

Jim thought, when he was a little boy, the world was filled with darkness and laws. Jim can't help but to think how quick we all fall.

Jim said that he didn't have much of a childhood, yet he still had fun. And it seemed to be good.

He thought that there's a question that most of us can ask; was I a good or bad child? Did he do his best? He knows that no one can choose the family that they are born into, but they must learn to do the things that they are supposed to do.

Jim wonders, *Do any of us know who we are or what journey we are going to take or how long we travel or how far?*

He thought, a father he didn't have, and his mother did her best. He was raised up no better or no worse than most the rest. He was taught that he had to go to school, and once he got there, he was expected to follow all of the rules. He wasn't the one that made all As, but he wasn't dumb; he still had decent grades.

Jim knows that some might turn to drinking, smoking, sex, or even religion to ease their pain; but when it all comes down, he thinks that we are all the same. But Jim knows that once we turn our lives over to Jesus, there is nothing in this life that can separate us. He knows that we are forgiven for our sins and that it's not our physical work that will get us in.

Jim knows that there is a heaven for those who truly believe, but he also knows that in this world, it can be so easy to be deceived. He hears the preachers say that we have to live our lives right, but in who's vision is this? In whose sight?

As a matter of fact, in this world, Jim sees us fighting many wars; but he knows that it doesn't matter because there's no one keeping any scores.

He sees boys and girls living in sin only because it feels good, and they're trying to fit in.

He sees a plant wither up and die simply because the soil is too hard and dry. The days are dark much like the night; soon, they say that you can forget about any sunlight.

In Jim's eyes, the world looks like it's ending, and he truly wonders if there will be a new beginning.

Jim knows that it doesn't matter how hard he tries; it will not be easy for him to say goodbye!

The Sea Captain

There was a certain captain that set sail for the sea; he had a small crew that was made up of only three.

He was asked, "Why are we setting sail for the sea? From what is it that you are trying to flee?"

The captain reluctantly looked at his ship and answered his crew; he told them, "If only you knew." He said, "I'm not one to express how I really feel, so I will try to do this without making it a big deal."

I had this lady; she was really out of sight. Just the thought of her could warm your coldest nights. Her skin was as soft as the clouds up above. I thought for sure that it was true love. But she said that this love just might not be, so now you know why we are casting out to the sea.

One of his crew members looked at the captain with curiosity in his eye; then he asked, "So you're just going to give up like this, and not even try? It appears to me, if I had a lady that was like a burning fire, one that could ignite my deepest desire, I wouldn't care if we were like two ships in the night. There would be no way that I would let her out of my sight."

The captain looked at his first mate and said, "You just don't understand, for you're just a simple man. I've done all that I could to make her mine. I've treated her with passion, and I've been ever so kind. I've taken her to the stores, and I let her shop; she shopped so much until she was ready to drop."

The old mate, with one patch over his eye, said, "I see what you've done. You've given it a try, but the feelings that you have, are they feelings that you can trust, or is it when you look at this lady, you're just filled with deep lust? What about the lady, when you look into her eyes, is there such a glow, or in her eyes, is the answer just no?"

With a growl on his face, the captain looked at his mate, "I never should have spoken with you. I should have known that you wouldn't be able to relate. You could never understand that there could be nothing worse than to lose or to leave the one whom you come to love first. Ships sailed underneath the clear blue skies, yet it's only her face that appears my eyes. You'll travel thousands of miles to witness her beautiful smile.

"No, how can you understand when you are but only a simple man.

"As the sun comes up to shine, I can only dream of the day that she will be mine, so as the clouds that floats high above, I can't wait for her to share this special love."

The mate held his head down to the deck. "Captain, I hate to crush your dreams. I hate to bring them to a wreck because the feelings that you have for her, in my mind, I don't doubt are true, but there is one question that I must ask, does she feel the same about you?"

The captain turned away from his first mate. "I thought that if I went out to sea, that when I returned, her feelings would have grown more for me. She looks at me as if I'm a pest even though I've given her my all. I've given her my best. I've given her diamonds, rubies, and pearls. I know that I'm not the best-looking fellow in the world, but all that I'm asking is for her to be my girl."

"Well, captain, I might be a simple fellow, but there is one thing that I do know. That is when love don't love you back, it's time to let it go."

Cyrus's Love Letter

I hope that this letter doesn't push you away, but there are some things that I've been meaning to say. From the moment that I looked into your eyes, your beauty, your smile, and your lips just got me hypnotized.

There have been so many days and nights that I've dreamed about you. I can't help but to hope and wonder if you have the same dreams too. I can search high and low. I can search all around the world. There could never be another woman for me; you are my girl.

When we first met, we were like two ships that pass through the night; but since I've gotten to know you, I never want to let you out of my sight. From the moment that you sunk into my arms, I wanted to fill you up with all of my charm. I was supposed to hold you for just one night, but for some reason, that just didn't exactly feel right. From the time of that very first kiss, I knew that if I let you go, you would be truly missed.

You know, when I first saw you, I thought that it was simply infatuation. I thought what I was feeling was just my own drawn-out lustful imagination, but now my love for you is just like the morning dew. I pray that you know and believe that my words are true. Even when I close my eyes, I can still see your face. I want you to know that no one could ever take your place.

Just like the stars that shine in the moonlit sky, my love for you will never die. The beauty that you have, I will always see; it doesn't matter what differences may come or how old we might be. I forever want to hold you close because it is you whom I love the most.

I told you that all I needed was just one night, and I would prove to you that I could take away all of your deepest frights.

When I look into your eyes, so big and round, everything else is blocked out. I ignore all other sounds. The twinkle in your eye is like a burning fire; deep down in me, you ignite such a burning desire. Your lips are as soft as the clouds above; just the touch of them made me fall deeply in love. You have such a beautiful smile, and the way you dress, you have an elegant style. And I love so much just to hear you talk, and I dare to mention your ever-so-sexy walk.

I can say that you're like an angel that was sent from above; you are someone that I would be thrilled to share all of my love. I tell you that I love you more and more each day. So we shouldn't let all of this passion just slip away.

I guess what I'm trying to say is that I never want to see you go because I know that deep in my heart, our love will continue to grow.

Watching The Grass

Carl was a strange type of guy; he would sometimes just sit and watch the grass and just cry. He often thought that he was going crazy, but others often thought that he was just plain old lazy. Some days, Carl would just get an old chair and just sit in the open field; he did this before he would take his pills.

One day, Carl went to the park. He got on his knees, and he started to talk. But the funny thing was he didn't talk to the people as they passed; instead, he was on his knees talking to the grass.

Carl just loved being outside; he said that that it had to feel like heaven after one had died.

Everyone that knew Carl said that he had a good heart; they said this before all of his craziness would start.

One morning, when Carl woke up, he walked around the room. It seemed to be filled with darkness; it seemed to be filled with gloom. Carl turned and looked at his bed, and what did he see? He thought, *Is this a silhouette, and it looks just like me?* He then thought to himself, *Am I being deceived? What is it? What am I to believe?*

He then continued doing the things that he had to do, but he couldn't help but to wonder, *What was for real? What was really true?*

He tried to run; he tried to hide. He finally came to the conclusion that he had died. All of a sudden, a light started to shine; was he going to heaven, or was he going to be left behind?

He tried to look back at all the things that he used to do, but he still didn't know; he still didn't have a clue.

All of a sudden, Carl opened his eyes; from a very deep sleep, he didn't know what to think, so he started to weep. Carl wondered how much time had passed, but he didn't give it too much thought; he started back watching the grass.

You see, Carl loved to watch the grass grow because in his mind, the grass was the only true friend that he had come to know. Carl even gave some of the grass names, but he would forget which was which because they all looked the same. He didn't really care because he loved them all, but the season that he didn't care too much for was the fall. He didn't care too much for how the grass would turn brown and the leaves would fall; he didn't like that his beautiful green grass wouldn't spring up when he would call.

Mooka's Story

Mooka laid down to sleep thinking about his week.

He was suddenly awakened and treated as if he was a freak; he was bound in chains as if he had neither mind nor brains. They put him so deep down in a boat; it was so hot and steaming, the odor made him choke. Mooka looked around to see all that he could see, but all he could see was darkness looking to see what it could see. They took him off the boat as if he was an animal; if he would had stayed any longer, he would have turned into a cannibal. They put him upon an action block as if he was poultry or even livestock; they looked at his arms, his legs, and his teeth. They looked at him as if he was a side of beef. Mooka followed a man who was pale as snow; he did not know where he would lead him, but he knew that he had to go. He looked at the others the same color as his eye, but they did not dare to speak; all they could do was to sigh.

He was forced up in the early dawn without his family, without his son; he prepared his mind for a very long trip, but each time he ran, they hit him on his back with a whip. Once again, he tried to run; he tried to take flight, but he did not know whom to turn to, for they all looked alike. At night, when he had time, he looked into the sky; he stared at the stars with tears in his eyes. He stood as a strong figure of a man but brokenhearted because all that he had known and loved were now departed.

Mooka wondered, *Why did they do this to me? They took away everything that I loved to see. When I arrived here, they called me wild, but they are the ones who stripped me away from my wife and child.*

He had to learn to deal with a lot of stress, which in no way was an easy task because each time, he slipped.

The taskmaster would laugh and crack his long, black, whip. They took his bright-skinned brothers, and they told all of them that they were not like the others; they told them that they were better than the rest until they slept with their daughters and disturbed their happiness.

They tried to take away Mooka's history; they wanted his past to become a complete mystery.

In God's name, in Jesus's name, he will always pray that in bondage, he will not always stay.

Just When You Thought You Knew

Printed in the United States
by Baker & Taylor Publisher Services